Lovett H. Weems, Jr.

The Right Questions

for Church Leaders

Abingdon Press™
Nashville

I0210867

THE RIGHT QUESTIONS FOR CHURCH LEADERS

Copyright © 2025 by Abingdon Press

All rights reserved.

No part of this work may be reproduced or transmitted in any form or by any means, electronic or mechanical, including photocopying and recording, or by any information storage or retrieval system, except as may be expressly permitted by the 1976 Copyright Act, the 1998 Digital Millennium Copyright Act, or in writing from the publisher. Requests for permission should be addressed to Abingdon Press, 810 12th Avenue South, Nashville, TN 37203 or emailed to permissions@abingdonpress.com.

978-1-7910-3701-7

Library of Congress Control Number has been requested.

Scripture quotations marked NRSVue are taken from the New Revised Standard Version Updated Edition. Copyright © 2021 National Council of Churches of Christ in the United States of America. Used by permission. All rights reserved worldwide.

Scripture quotations marked CEB are taken from the Common English Bible, copyright 2011. Used by permission. All rights reserved.

MANUFACTURED IN THE UNITED STATES OF AMERICA

Praise for *The Right Questions for Church Leaders*

"In times of uncertainty, it is human nature to reach for answers. Dr. Weems reminds us how essential it is that we instead ask questions: of ourselves, each other, and the systems in which we serve and live. In asking, we express curiosity that invites the Holy Spirit; and in listening, we make connections that allow us to find the best way forward. In this season of uncertainty, this book is a gift to every leader who loves the church and wants it to thrive."
—Elizabeth Garrigan-Byerly, Executive Minister for Area Conference Ministry, Southern New England Conference, United Church of Christ

"Lovett Weems is widely regarded as one of the most respected voices in the church today, particularly in leadership teaching and coaching. *The Right Questions for Church Leaders* is an essential resource, presented as a well-equipped toolbox filled with invaluable tools for effective leadership. Written by a true master builder, this book offers practical insights and guidance. Exploring its pages, I found myself selecting specific topics and uncovering the perfect 'word-tool' to address a given challenge that may need tightening up, fixing in some way, or made to be more effective and productive."
—Stan Copeland, senior pastor, Lovers Lane United Methodist Church, Dallas, TX

"Lovett Weems beautifully leads the reader into contemplation about their own lives and their legacy of leadership in this practical and engaging book. As pastors navigate an uncertain ecclesial future, these questions will help them move forward effectively. This is a much-needed resource."
—Camille Cook Howe, senior pastor, Georgetown Presbyterian Church, Washington, DC

"With his usual pastoral wisdom and warmth, Weems offers this collection of questions to guide church leaders in these complex and challenging times. As I read this book, I kept stopping to reflect on how I, our staff, and our members would respond to these important and revealing questions. This book will be a valuable tool for church staff and leadership boards as they discern current realities and vision for future effectiveness in ministry."
—Amy Aitken, pastor, First United Methodist Church, Pasadena, CA

"This practical, relevant, and timely resource equips leaders to be life-long learners, moving toward greater personal and social transformation. As a leader of leaders, I appreciate and highly recommend this compilation of wisdom. From its reading, I will become more intentional about integrating this practice of curiosity into my leadership, and share the practice with other leaders."
—Aleze M. Fulbright, district superintendent, Indiana Conference, UMC

To read a new Right Question each week in the free online newsletter
of the Lewis Center for Church Leadership, subscribe to
Leading Ideas at www.churchleadership.com.

Other Abingdon Press Books by Lovett H. Weems, Jr.

High Yield: Seven Disciplines of the Fruitful Leader (with Tom Berlin)

Overflow: Increase Worship Attendance & Bear More Fruit (with Tom Berlin)

Focus: The Real Challenges That Face The United Methodist Church

Bearing Fruit: Ministry with Real Results (with Tom Berlin)

Church Leadership: Vision, Team, Culture, and Integrity, Revised Edition

The Crisis of Younger Clergy (with Ann A. Michel)

Take the Next Step: Leading Lasting Change in the Church

Leadership in the Wesleyan Spirit

John Wesley's Message Today

Leaders do not need answers.
Leaders must have the right questions.

Contents

Contents

Contents

Introduction

Andrew Young was mayor of Atlanta, a congressman from Georgia, and U.S. ambassador to the United Nations. But before all those positions, he was a United Church of Christ clergy and civil rights leader who was one of the closest associates of Martin Luther King, Jr. Young tells of joining Dr. King for a meeting with President Lyndon Johnson about the need for a voting rights bill. As the two of them left the White House, King recalled a previous meeting he had with Johnson's predecessor, John F. Kennedy. "Kennedy asked questions for an hour," King remarked, "Johnson talks for an hour. That's the difference between them."[1]

Fortunately, President Johnson's leadership included other skills and relationships that resulted in the passage of historic civil rights and voting rights bills. But Dr. King's incisive observation reflects the truth about most great leaders. The practice of asking questions so easily practiced in our preschool years gives way to reticence as we grow older. We grow out of practice and assume that others are as reluctant to respond to questions as we are to ask them. Quite the opposite is the case. Few things bring more satisfaction to someone than to be asked something about which they have knowledge or experience. Assuming that others have valuable insights is a way of honoring the other person.

Every year fewer leaders can accomplish goals merely by announcing them. Using the authority of a position to accomplish things is less and less effective, even in traditional hierarchical organizations. Command has given way to collaboration for the most effective modern leaders. Wise and effective church leaders are certainly learning this lesson. However, positions of leadership are not powerless. Perhaps the greatest benefit of positional power is the ability to convene and to propose discussion agendas. Persons in positions of leadership have access to virtually everyone in the organization. Clergy know this. They can raise almost any questions related to the church's mission. They can share information from such discussions across the congregation as a way of encouraging learning and further collaboration.

But most leaders need more practice in developing and asking the kinds of questions that draw usefully from the wisdom of their colleagues and constituents. Our hope is that this collection of questions will provide church leaders the help they need as they face particular challenges. One of the questions found here may be just what one needs in a situation. Just as likely, one of these questions will trigger another question that fits your context even better. As you use these questions, you will become more skilled in developing your own questions and finding unexpected opportunities to use questioning in a multitude of daily settings.

Having an answer may be useful, but having the right questions is where creativity and innovation begin.

—Lovett H. Weems, Jr.

Reflections on Question Asking

Why Ask Questions?

The leader of the past was a person who knew how to tell. The leader of the future will be a person who knows how to ask.

—Peter Drucker[1]

We know that leaders spend most of their time communicating with others in numerous ways. However, most of that communication involves telling instead of asking. David Brooks observes that about 30 percent of people in his experience tend to be "question askers."[2] That is unfortunate since question asking opens immense opportunities for leaders—for leadership is always about the group, not about the leader.

As one wise educator wrote, "My teaching and consulting experience has taught me that what builds a relationship, what solves problems, what moves things forward is asking *the right questions*."[3] To be effective, leaders must first bond with their coworkers and constituents. Nothing builds solid relationships more than asking appropriate questions that honor the wisdom others possess.

Always keep in mind that asking questions and listening is not a political act to gain support. It is a practice that will test your integrity. Leaders do not need to act on everything they hear. No one expects that. But once you ask people to invest in addressing your questions, then you have an obligation to take those ideas seriously and to show some evidence that their ideas matter. They will understand when you are not always able to do what many people want, but they will be well served by your acknowledging the differences rather than acting as if their ideas were never considered. Perhaps the greatest untapped power in any organization is found in the unknown ideas and insights of all those in a wide range of roles in the group.

Personal Reflection and Growth

As important as engagement with others is for leaders, there must also be time for self-reflection. Good leaders seek feedback, and all leaders receive feedback, whether they recognize it or not. However, leaders must assess themselves and their leadership periodically based on what they know about their performance and about themselves.

PERSONAL REFLECTION QUESTIONS

We all have commitments, values, and responsibilities that we like to think we are upholding. Robin Diangelo suggests a question we would do well to ask about these things we consider important:

How do I know how I am doing?

Pastor John Mark Comer came to a time in his ministry when he realized that he had to simplify and focus what he was doing. The question that came to him while on an airplane flight that led to change is one that has challenged people of faith for generations:

What if I changed my life?

Saj-nicole A. Joni reminds leaders not to think too narrowly about their work but to ask questions such as:

> Does this agenda cover the full picture?
> Am I leaving the right legacy?

———————

James R. Hagerty writes obituaries for the *Wall Street Journal*. He urges everyone to write a draft of their own obituary and, in the process, write a longer life story for your family. He suggests three questions:

> What were you trying to do with your life?
> Why?
> And how did it work out?

———————

Dr. Jacqueline Lewis, pastor of Middle Collegiate Church in New York City, proposes we think of life as a story in progress. Her suggested questions include:

> If your life were a book, what is the title of the book?
> What's the title of the current chapter?
> What are the titles of the chapters that got you here?
> What do you want the end of your story—
> the last chapter—to be titled?
> What chapters do you need to "write" to get to that
> final chapter?

———————

Many have noted that a leader's demeanor often sets the tone for a group. Edwin Friedman talked about how a leader's "anxious presence" is picked up by others and thus encouraged leaders to practice a "non-anxious presence." With that in mind, it may help to ask yourself this question:

> If my emotional state is contagious,
> what will those around me catch?

INTEGRITY QUESTIONS

Theologian Hans Küng wrote that members of any group, ecclesial or not, are always vitally interested in the following, without which leadership cannot function and a credibility gap arises:

> Does the leader really believe what he or she says?
> Is the leader convinced that the road to which the leader points
> is the right one?
> Does the leader regard the proposed goal as attainable?

_____

Christians should never despair and think that positive change is impossible. Carlos Correa Bernier reminds believers that what appears complex and overwhelming must drive us back to the most elemental questions of our faith and character as well as what we believe about the future. His questions are:

> What is it that I believe?
> And what am I going to do about it?

_____

The following is a soul-searching question that helps us explore what others think of us as well as our basic integrity as a church:

Are there areas in which we say one thing but do another?

———————

For leaders to make a difference, they must have a passion for the cause they are leading. Rosabeth Moss Kanter suggests questions to see if you pass the "passion test" for the effort you seek to lead.

Does the idea fit my long-held beliefs, values, and convictions?
Do I think that this is vital for the future of people I care about?
Do I get excited when I think about it and
convey excitement when I talk about it?
Am I convinced this can be accomplished?

BECOMING A BETTER LEADER QUESTIONS

Justin Irving and Mark Strauss say that when problems arise in an organization, leaders must model what matters when it comes to vulnerable self-evaluation. Ask yourself the tough questions:

How am I contributing to this issue or problem?
Are there areas of my inner life that adversely affect my work or
those with whom I work?
Are there any personal blind spots I'm missing in the situation?
Do I need to seek out insight from anyone who could help me
see these blind spots?

———————

Both individual leaders and congregations can benefit from identifying things that we do that others find important and are appreciated. There are other practices that we might do from time to time but often are not attentive enough to doing. These questions may help:

> What are some things that we should do more consistently?
> How will we do that?

———

Canadian pastor Carey Nieuwhof offers a series of questions to help leaders gain momentum in their leadership, including the following:

> In your weekly routine, what are you having
> to manufacture energy to do?
> How can you put more fuel in the areas
> that are seeing the most traction?

———

Carey Nieuwhof also offers these questions that may be helpful for a quick checkup on how you are doing as a leader:

> Is anyone following you?
> If no one's following, you are not leading.
> Who is following you?
> High-capacity leaders will attract other high-capacity people.
> Who are you following?
> Who's mentoring you?
> With whom do you spend time?

Gaining Perspective

All organizations have unique cultures, and churches have an identity that takes shape early. Leaders must understand this identity; change and growth flow more effectively when such change emerges out of this identity or "DNA." Congregations also exist within specific local contexts, and appropriate leadership will be attentive to the context. But the longer we are a part of a church, the more immersed we may become in its culture and less able to experience church life as new people do. One of the most difficult yet essential tasks for leaders is to see their churches as others see them.

UNDERSTANDING YOUR CHURCH'S IDENTITY QUESTIONS

All institutions are dealing with their past these days. Congregations often discover there were seasons in their histories when their witness was not in alignment with what they believe today to be God's will. An issue of *Alban Weekly* offered excellent questions for churches to use in reflecting on their history:

What story or time period from our congregation's past
do we highlight when we tell our history?
What is it about that story or period that makes us celebrate it?
What is the story or time period from our history
that we skip over in telling our story?
What is it about that story or period that we would
rather ignore?

Churches within a community may appear quite similar. They do share common characteristics. But people experience churches very differently. Two questions can help us think about what distinguishes our church:

> What is the distinctive contribution our church
> makes to our community?
> With all the similarities among churches, what differentiates us?

———————

Some churches are wondering if their church name still fits. Shawn Stewart offers six questions for churches to consider before renaming the church:

> Why do we want to rename our church?
> What is our church's history?
> Where are we headed?
> What common themes seem to repeat in the life of our church?
> What kind of names are we drawn to?
> How could our new name be interpreted negatively?

———————

Churches that set themselves apart as distinctive in some way tend to grow more than churches that people view in a more generic way. Finding what might be a special focus for your church needs to connect with your mission and tradition while at the same time setting itself apart from many or most other churches. One question that may help this discernment is:

> What is a need that fits our mission and capabilities that no
> other church is addressing and is not likely to begin addressing?

———————

A future vision has a much greater chance of succeeding if anchored in a congregation's history and values. James Harnish provides two excellent questions for thinking ahead:

> What stories from the past can help define your congregation's ministry in the future?
> Who are the people who can help you get in touch with the roots of your congregation?

UNDERSTANDING YOUR CONTEXT QUESTIONS

According to Kay Kotan and Blake Bradford, these questions can help a congregation align its vision to its mission field:

> Who are we as a congregation now?
> Who is our neighbor?
> What is the gap between our congregation and our mission field?
> What must we do, give up, and/or change to reach our neighbors for Christ?

Lee Kricher suggests that churches ask this question among their members to get their impressions and then turn to recent census data to determine what the reality is:

> Generally, how do you think the average age of the people who attend our church compares with the average age of the people in the surrounding community?

Several congregations have asked a variety of members to spend time in their communities simply paying attention to what they experience. They have discovered that this process can provide new clues for a more relevant ministry. Alan J. Roxburgh suggests going for a 45-minute walk with observation questions, such as:

What do you see? Not see?
What do you smell? Not smell?
What do you hear? Not hear?
What do you feel? Not feel?
What effect did any of these things have on you?
Did you stop to listen to anyone on your walks?

In planning for another year, whether for program or budgeting, it is easy to design plans modeled after the most recent year. Consider, instead, taking time to think about the lives of those you seek to serve as the background for that planning. Possible questions include:

What has changed in the lives of our members
in the last three to five years?
What changes are they facing in the next three to five years?

There are always more good ideas than any church can implement, so deciding among good options is a regular challenge. One question that may help before embarking on a new program is:

What is the need this program addresses and to what extent is it
felt by those we are seeking to reach?

As you think about people your church is seeking to reach and serve, Rich Birch suggests these questions:

> What questions are people asking, and how do we
> answer those as a church?
> What are the things that people are struggling with
> for which our church could help?
> What are the things that people wonder about
> that we should be discussing?

SEEING YOUR CHURCH
AS OTHERS DO QUESTIONS

Most churches have traffic passing by their facilities each day. Roman Catholic priest Michael White suggests a question all churches should consider:

> Does your church look like it is open?

———————

Laura Everett, executive director of the Massachusetts Council of Churches, thinks churches are so focused on those already attending that they are insensitive to how church is experienced by others. This question can help:

> What does this look like for someone who has
> never opened a Bible, never opened a hymnal,
> never walked through a church door?

———————

Someone reported that in their congregation a provocative and deeply moving conversation took place when these two questions were asked to explore members' experience with the church:

> When were you most proud to be a member of this church?
> When were you so upset that you almost left?

———————

Greg Atkinson functions as a "secret shopper" for congregations to help them see their churches from the perspective of a newcomer. He suggests that many new people are asking these four questions when they enter your church:

> Where am I supposed to go?
> Where are my kids supposed to go?
> Where is the bathroom?
> Is there coffee?

———————

Church leaders would do well to think about those they serve with two questions:

> If someone asked the people of the congregation about us,
> what are some good and bad things they might say?
> Is there truth to what they are saying, including the good
> as well as the bad?

———————

Having good questions to ask newly active people in the church can help identify common practices that may have downsides about which church leaders are unaware. One question that can help is:

> Since attending church here, has anything made you feel uncomfortable or uneasy?

KNOWING WHAT'S GOING ON QUESTIONS

In times of rapid change, it is more important than ever to learn from what is happening. Even in times of chaos, says Gil Rendle, there are observations and clues that reflection and questioning can bring out. Such learning should be followed by this question he suggests:

> What now will we do with this?

Charles Zech, a Roman Catholic scholar, suggests two questions to understand your congregation better:

> Tell me about the overall quality of your parish. Would you describe it as: Above Average? Average? or Below Average?
> (No matter what the response is, ask this second question:)
> How do you know?

By the time problems are noticed by the wider community, much damage has already been done. By the time the entire membership realizes that the youth ministry has dwindled to one or two youth, the neglect that led to the decline has hurt the congregation's ministry beyond quick repair. Thus, leaders do well always to pay attention, using a question such as:

> What is going on behind the scenes that could be unraveling a ministry of our church?

Reflections on Question Asking

Questions Build Trust

The greatest compliment was paid to me today. Someone asked me what I thought and actually attended to my answer.

—Henry David Thoreau[1]

Trust is the currency of leadership. "People will only permit themselves to be questioned by those they trust. That means they can only be really led by those they trust," says ethicist Robin Lovin.[2] Trust is a requirement for questioning, but the practice of asking questions actually builds trust. Your questions communicate trust and invite trust. David Brooks thinks of questioning as a moral practice. "When you are asking a good question, you are adopting a posture of humility. You're confessing that you don't know, and you want to learn. You're also honoring a person," he says.[3] Much of his own use of questions has the effect of beginning or deepening a relationship.

Building trust begins not only with the content of the question but with how you present yourself and handle your questions. Beginning with the right tone, words, facial expressions, and physical space setup all matter. If the subject matter is such that you fear you may communicate something negative unintentionally based on some of the responses, then take notes as a way both to honor what the respondents are saying and making sure you keep a neutral posture even if some of the words are personally hurtful or feel unfair.

Making Good Decisions

Making decisions goes with leadership. Not many of those decisions are made apart from the help of others, for leadership decisions must consider far more than one's personal preference. Leaders serve within a context and are stewards of a larger mission, both of which have claims on their decision-making. The world of leaders is filled with challenges that stand between the current reality and successfully achieving our mission and goals. Challenges are a given, but leaders choose how they handle them. There will be differences and conflict, but leaders need not fear these situations. The goal is to engage differences in ways that affirm all people and their perspectives while still making progress toward common goals.

WISE JUDGMENT QUESTIONS

Andy Stanley offers several questions to guide our living. He calls one the "maturity question" to use whenever we face a decision:

> In light of your future hopes and dreams,
> what is the wise thing for you?

Leaders face times when they need to decide to stay with what they are doing or to move to some other place or role. Ursula M. Burns, former CEO of Xerox, when facing such a decision, was helped by a question she was asked by a colleague:

> Are you running away from something
> or running toward something?

Good leaders avoid unwise and unilateral actions that tend to provoke and polarize. However, most leadership requires movement before all uncertainty is gone. Mary Parker Follett, a leadership writer from the early twentieth century, encouraged leaders to heed the "law of the situation" that combines action *and* continuing feedback. Her question was:

> How do I accept and act on the reality of the situation
> as we are constantly in the process of understanding it
> in interaction with others?

Jeff Bezos distinguishes two types of decisions that leaders face. "One-way doors" are consequential and irreversible and require slow and careful consideration. On the other hand, most decisions are "two-way doors," in which, if things do not work out, you can regroup without great harm. Leaders may need to speed up the two-door decisions while slowing down the one-door decisions. So, a question to ask of each decision:

> Is this a one-way door decision or a two-way door decision?

Churches are reluctant to dampen enthusiasm that members have in wanting to take on a new ministry or project. However, often well-meaning people with the best of intentions move forward to help without doing enough homework. The result can be insensitivity and ineffectiveness in helping those they intend to serve. A question that can help encourage more conversation and investigation, without discouraging those interested in helping, can be:

> What more will we need to learn to do this well?

Starting something new is risky at best. One way to reduce uncertainty and rely less on luck and more on prudent planning is to ask good questions, such as:

On what facts is our plan based?
What assumptions are we making in our plan?
How can we test our most critical assumptions?
What are the weak parts of our plan?

FACING CHALLENGES QUESTIONS

Molly Phinney Baskette has written an insightful memoir of joy and enriching ministry in the midst of much suffering and loss. Her significant story, entitled *How to Begin When Your World is Ending*, is best captured in its subtitle, *A Spiritual Field Guide to Joy Despite Everything*. She names two questions central for her and for many people:

How much can we heal from the hard things that happen to us?
How do we find meaning and purpose from our woundings?

Congregations always have worries, but they are best faced forthrightly. George Thompson offers two questions to help:

What is the congregation most afraid of?
What has it done to address this fear?

Three writers on leadership (Susan MacKenty Brady, Janet Foutty, and Lynn Perry Wooten) address the dilemma we have when we want to appear competent but do not know what to do. They suggest reaching out to others with questions such as:

Will you help me?
Will you help me think through what we should do about this?

_____

It is easy to let problems worsen by neglect while focusing on other and easier subjects. Hayim Herring and Terri Martinson Elton pose these questions to help churches discover if they face this dilemma:

Are you a part of a congregation that has regularly scheduled meetings with reappearing agenda items?
Do critical issues languish for months at a time because they are not given due focus?

_____

Julia Binder and Michael D. Watkins suggest that when facing a tough problem, reframing the issue in a broader perspective can help—much as one might "zoom out" on a map to see a larger context in which a place is located. Using four categories developed by Lee Bolman and Terrence Deal, they offer these sets of questions:

Structural—How is the issue related to our formal structure, processes, and policies?
Human Resources—How does the issue impact people, relationships, and teamwork?
Political—How does the issue relate to power dynamics, competing interests, and patterns of influence?
Symbolic—How does the issue relate to our traditions, stories, shared values, and culture?

DEALING WITH DIFFERENCES QUESTIONS

David E. Smith is a philosopher whose goal is "to empower people to think for themselves about things that matter." In a lecture on "Civil Conversation in an Angry Age," he addressed two provocative questions, as reported by Mónica Guzmán:

> Are you willing to believe that you are wrong about something?
> Which do you value more: the truth or your own beliefs?

———————

Often when we work regularly with those who don't share our views, there can be a tendency to focus on those differences. Chloe Maxmim and Canyon Woodward suggest that a better beginning point is to identify those things that we share, using a question such as:

> What are our common hopes, dreams, fears, and frustrations?

———————

In a polarized time when opinions seem fixed, and few want to hear ideas different from their own (whether it's about vaccinations, politics, or religion), standoffs quickly arise. Research shows how difficult it is to change the mind of another person. One question suggested by Adam Grant is:

> What evidence would change your mind?

———————

Mónica Guzmán works with people having polarized views to help them communicate across their differences to foster greater understanding. She says if there is one question people should ask far more often than we do, it would be:

> What am I missing?

CONFLICT QUESTIONS

Church historian Justo L. González suggests we adopt a more realistic view of history, focusing more on what we can learn than on naming "good guys and bad guys." Instead of merely asking who was right, he urges attention to questions such as:

> What were the forces—social, economic, religious—at play in a
> given conflict, and how did they help determine the outcome?
> How do we discern God's will in such a history
> without heroes or saints?
> How do we discern God's will in our own days
> when a similar history is unfolding?

When there is an impasse in a contentious debate, a compromise is found, often one with which no one is pleased. Thomas G. Kirkpatrick suggests questions to ask before moving to compromise, including:

> What is the primary issue about which we are differing?
> What are the goals we each seek?
> What other options do we have?

A pastor tells about a clergy mentor who worked with him during the early years of ministry. Often when the new pastor was describing some particularly troublesome dilemma from the congregation, the mentor had a way of asking a question that caused the pastor to view the situation very differently. The question was:

Is this more about you or about them?

_____

When someone brings up a disturbing trend or other negative assessment, responses often are defensive or blaming. Perhaps this question can move the conversation in a different direction:

How do we know that, and how can we learn more?

Working with Others

Leadership is always about a group and never the leader. Progress comes from working with the many others to fulfill the mission and take that next faithful step. A strong, gifted, growing, and trained cadre of leaders is essential for ongoing vitality; thus, one of a leader's most important tasks is to identify and support new emerging leaders. At the same time, even the most dedicated and dependable existing leaders need care and encouragement. Working with others also entails meetings, which many leaders do not enjoy. But meetings can be channels of creativity and productivity if approached thoughtfully. Think of a meeting as a task with a purpose, values, and goals.

ENGAGING OTHERS QUESTIONS

Debi Nixon talks about how easy it is for most of us, even those with the best of intentions, to move toward those with whom we are most comfortable. She has found a question that helps her resist this tendency when she enters a setting:

> Who is in the room that maybe no one else has noticed?

———————

Knowing that people are our greatest asset and that the issues we face today are exceedingly complex, Hayim Herring and Terri Martinson Elton suggest a distinctive stance for congregations through this question:

> What if congregations flipped their understanding of themselves
> from being dispensers of information to platforms
> for collective learning?

———————

Rick Rusaw and Brian Mavis encourage positive questions when first getting to know new people. They suggest:

> What are you good at?
> What skills do you have?
> What energizes you?

———————

It is common for church leaders to be asked a question such as, "Tell me about your church." The temptation is to tell your practiced standard story. However, think about how that experience might change if, instead, you replied with this question:

> What would be most useful for you to know about our church?

IDENTIFYING LEADERS QUESTIONS

One of the key roles for pastoral leaders is to "equip the saints for the work of ministry" (Ephesians 4:12) and to develop new leaders throughout the congregation. Lee Kricher uses a question that can help pastors assess how they are doing:

> Would the people in your congregation who know you best consider you to be a leader who is deeply committed to developing other leaders and sharing leadership?

Carey Nieuwhof suggests seven questions that "every volunteer asks but never says out loud." Make sure you have good answers to all of these before making your next request for service:

> Is this really about the mission?
> Are the relationships around here healthy?
> Will serving help me grow spiritually?
> Am I just a means to an end?
> Will you help me develop the skills I need?
> Are you organized, or are you going to waste my time?
> Am I signing up for life?

Robert Schnase suggests that we may be asking new participants in our churches the wrong questions. Instead of asking them on which committee they would like to serve, better questions might be:

Tell me about a ministry you have felt God calling you to fulfill.
What difference do you feel God is calling you to make?
What gifts and skills and passions do you have for ministry?

———————

Churches do much better today in helping members discern their ministries in the church and community based on their gifts rather than merely filling positions needed by the church. Questions that may help you understand where God is calling you or others include:

What brings you joy?
What can you do as well as just about anyone?
What tasks bring you satisfaction?
What do other people say you are good at doing?
What things do you enjoy doing so much
that you lose track of time?

LEADING GROUPS QUESTIONS

In *Miseducated: A Memoir*, Brandon Fleming tells the remarkable story of his personal transformation as well as about his work with urban youth who achieved at the highest levels of the summer Harvard Debate Council. Fleming told the youth that his measure of success for them is captured in one question:

How did you make someone else's life better?

———————

Staff teams and other work groups might find these questions helpful in assessing how they function:

> Are we committed to a common purpose?
> Are we committed to one another?
> Do we adapt as needed?
> Do we engage conflict that arises?

Donna Claycomb Sokol and L. Roger Owens suggest excellent questions for use at the end of a study time or meeting:

> Where have we sensed God's Spirit leading us
> in this conversation?
> Where was there hope and energy?
> Where do we need God's guidance as we move forward
> in this area of church life?
> For what do we have to give thanks for our time together?
> Did an obvious next step emerge?

Churches and their leaders deal with good ideas, suggestions, and proposals that are filled with the best of intentions. But sometimes there are flaws in the logic behind the cause-and-effect assumptions imbedded in these proposals. Virtually all proposals recommend that the church do x in order for y to happen. Therefore, one question that can help test the logic of the proposal is:

> How do you know?

MAKING THE MOST OF MEETINGS QUESTIONS

Leaders are often surprised to discover how much time they spend talking in meetings, including meetings called to invite the opinions of others. Leaders should regularly ask after meetings:

> Did I talk too much?
> How can I give others more time to share?

———————

Jessica Anschutz tells of a practice she found helpful as a pastor to bring the tone of church meetings more in alignment with the spiritual focus of the congregation. The opening question that brought good energy and focus to the meeting's work was:

> How have you witnessed God at work since we last met?

———————

Eric Hoeke suggests that church teams and committees use their first meeting of the year, or the one at which new group members are first present, to set guidelines for how they will work together. Some call this a behavioral covenant. These questions may help:

> How shall we work together?
> What can we count on from each other?
> How will we handle differences?

———————

Leaders often convene meetings of teams, staff, task groups, and committees. Good leaders understand the group's tasks and come prepared with an agenda to accomplish those tasks. Sometimes, a good leader thinks further about the group's work thus far and asks these questions:

> What is something good this group has made possible?
> How can we celebrate this accomplishment
> to begin the meeting?

_____

Think about the agenda for your governing board or a committee on which you serve and ask these questions:

> What items are always on the agenda?
> What items are rarely or never on the agenda?
> What does that say about our priorities
> and possible missing items?

_____

One way to make meetings you lead more productive and fulfilling for everyone is to go into each meeting thinking of the two questions Thomas G. Kirkpatrick says most people enter a meeting asking:

> Why are we meeting?
> How may I participate?

Reflections on Question Asking

Right Questions Help Communicate Values and Priorities

Asking questions is one of the most important tools we as organizers have at our disposal. Asking questions is how we get to know what's underneath and in between our experiences in communities.

—Alicia Garza[1]

Communicating values and priorities through questions is far different from convincing others to accept your agenda and priorities. Leaders use questions to ascertain existing values and loyalties, while at the same time helping to discern together the shape of the current situation and what may be good directions for the future. The goal is not to win a debate but to discover common understandings and goals.

Once goals and values are clear, then your questions can be in alignment with those future goals. James Kouzes suggests that leaders do an audit of their questions. Keep track of the questions you ask in various settings. "Do these questions help clarify and gain commitment to shared values?" asks Kouzes.[2] The questions you ask say much about what is important.

If you are asking about a particular aspect of your organization, you are communicating your interest to those in that group. This may be a component of the organization that has been undervalued by others. If you are asking for suggestions about how some particular goals can be best achieved in this component, you are reminding everyone that these goals are important.

The film producer Brian Grazer has built his leadership and creativity around asking questions as a way of life. He believes that questions "can quietly transmit values more powerfully than a direct statement telling people what you want them to stand for or exhorting them about what you want them to stand for."[3] This is a good reminder that not all questions are equally helpful. Since so many leaders spend most of their time telling instead of asking, when they do ask questions, often they are asked in a way that comes across as more advocating than inquiring, as Peter Senge has noted. Senge observes that in many organizations, ninety percent of the questions asked are not questions at all but "statements disguised as questions."[4]

Making a Difference

Leaders want to make a difference. That's part of the challenge of positions of responsibility. Leaders have a chance to guide, motivate, set agendas, and make life better for many people. The best leaders think beyond what is required by their job descriptions and dream of how things can be better because of their efforts.

RESULTS-BASED LEADERSHIP QUESTIONS

One thing that distinguishes the biblical model of fruitful leadership is that there is always a desired harvest. All efforts keep in mind a future destination or outcome. Important questions are:

Have we reached the desired outcome?
If not, how far along the journey have we come?

"For God so loved the world" begins a treasured passage of scripture. Churches need to remember that they exist to serve that same world to which God sent Jesus Christ. A question that helps us remember is:

What is different in the world because of our work?

Having good measures for the outcomes (fruits) you seek is important. Having the right measures is even more important. Questions to consider before determining *what you need to monitor* include:

Is it influenceable?
Can it be measured?
Is it worth measuring?

When considering the launching of a new ministry, try using these questions Tony Morgan suggests:

Do we know what type of good fruit we expect?
If so, will the new ministry produce it?

With churches more attentive to the fruitfulness of their efforts, Howard Stevenson suggests questions appropriate for almost any ministry group:

How do you define success?
How do you track it?

The biblical image of fruitfulness triggers natural questions for leaders:

Is the fruitfulness you seek right for your location?
What have you learned from others seeking
such fruitfulness in your area?
Do you understand the ecosystem that produces
this fruitfulness for others?
Have you prepared the soil so as to have reason
to expect a fruitful harvest?

PRIORITIES QUESTIONS

In the early days of Martin Luther King, Jr.'s Southern Christian Leadership Conference, legendary civil rights organizer Ella Baker volunteered to help bring order to the many initiatives going on at any one time. After her review, she provided a question rather than a solution:

Have we been so busy doing the things that had to be done
that we have failed to do what should be done?

_____

When leaders are seeking to accomplish a major project or produce important results, several questions are likely to be helpful:

Where should I spend my time?
With whom should I meet?
What new information do I need?

_____

James Harnish provides a good question to keep our attention focused on our current responsibilities:

> What is God calling us to do or to be in this place
> at this moment with these people?

———————

John Perkins is an evangelical Bible teacher and community developer. He combines a passion for souls and for society, a combination he sees essential for Christians. Therefore, a question he has used for himself and others is:

> What is God's program on earth, and how do I fit in?

———————

A few years ago, the Lewis Center for Church Leadership staff were all asked to respond to four questions as a way of determining the shape of the Center's next chapter. Perhaps these questions can help in other settings:

> Raise? What acts and activities could profitably be raised
> above their current level?
> Reduce? What acts and activities could be reduced
> from the current level of time and energy?
> Eliminate? What acts and activities could be eliminated?
> Add? What things could we do that we are not now doing that,
> if done well, would take us to new levels of mission effectiveness?

———————

There are many ways to determine priorities for effort, time, and finances. One question that many find helpful is:

> Where and in what ways can we change lives most profoundly?

MAKING AN IMPACT QUESTIONS

There are more good ideas than any church or church leader can pursue. The challenge is sorting out the ones that will matter most. One question that may provide guidance is:

> To what extent will this help those we serve?

Charles Zech, a retired Villanova professor, encourages congregations to focus more carefully on what they are accomplishing. Questions that he suggests include:

> How will we know when we are accomplishing our mission?
> How will we know that we have impacted our parishioners?
> How will we know how effective the church staff is?
> How will we know if our programs are effective?
> How will we know how to allocate our financial resources?

The late Bishop Gerald Kennedy told of someone who suggested that the question he would have to answer at the Last Judgment was:

> Well, what did you make of it?

Sometimes groups complain about things that cannot be changed or at least not in the near future. It may be an ineffective staff member still a few years from retirement or inadequate parking with no funds for more. In such situations, there are options other than despair. One is captured in this question:

> Given this reality, what can we do to make things better *now*?

———————

Someone asks to talk with you on a topic about which you know a great deal. The conversation could easily move toward all you know rather than what piece of what you know is most needed by the person coming to visit. A question to focus the conversation on the needs of the other person might be:

> What outcome would make this conversation a success for you?

BUILDING ON STRENGTHS QUESTIONS

You will learn a great deal about how members of your congregation view their church by using this question:

> If you could tell a new resident only one thing
> about your church, what would it be?

———————

Peter Drucker liked to ask two questions he considered important and that even successful people often cannot answer:

> Do you know what you're good at?
> Do you know what you need to learn so that you get
> the full benefit of your strengths?

———————

It is easy to become preoccupied with what our churches are lacking. Our attention gravitates to those missing pieces whether it is people, money, youth, or facilities. However, God has blessed all churches with gifts we often overlook. Try looking for potential promise for the future by using this question:

> What are assets we have in abundance, and how might
> they be used to bless and serve others?

———————

How your church is known in the community is very important in reaching new people. Often those active in another church will suggest your church to new people because they know enough about your church to know that the fit will be better for the newcomers. With that in mind, consider using these questions:

> For what is your church most known in the community?
> What are two or three things most people in the community
> know about your church?

Review and Assessment

All ministry begins with clarity about a church's purpose, and thus renewed vitality always begins with a rediscovered understanding of why your congregation exists. Over the years, the primacy of mission may recede amidst the work of keeping all the church activities going; therefore, all programs and activities need regular review in light of the church's purpose. Programs emerge to meet certain needs, and sometimes those needs change without consequent changes in programs. Leaders find ongoing ways to review all programs. Developing a culture of review and assessment with careful attention to appropriate metrics can contribute to a church that stays fresh and relevant.

A CHURCH'S PURPOSE QUESTIONS

Decisions are sometimes hard to make, especially when the discussion focuses solely on the merits of the proposed activity or change. Such deliberations can be helped by viewing the new effort in relationship to the larger picture of the church's calling with a question such as:

> In what ways will this advance the mission of our church?

_____

Churches can find themselves spending more and more time and energy on things relatively unrelated to their core mission. Here is *another approach* to asking whether our work is advancing our mission: First, name and clarify the stated mission. Second, list *all* church activities. Then you can be prepared to *rank or score them* by using an "advancing our mission" question:

> To what extent does this effort (this activity or program)
> contribute to advancing our mission?

_____

A church had no trouble beginning new things, but often the new activities stretched their capabilities. Some wondered if all the endeavors fit the church's purpose. A method that helped the church decide on future

37

initiatives was always to keep their mission statement before them and, in light of it, to ask of any proposal:

Should we do it?

_____

When Anne L. Bryant was executive director of the American Association of University Women, she used four questions to keep the organization focused on its mission as it considered new initiatives:

Is this needed?
Is it credible for us to do?
Do our members want it?
What can we uniquely contribute?

_____

Alicia Garza says that the potential of any movement for change is shaped by four questions:

Where are we?
Who are we?
From where did we come?
What do we care about most in the here and now?

REVIEWING PROGRAMS QUESTIONS

Rich Birch suggests three questions church leaders should be asking:

What things that worked at one point are no longer working?
What are we doing that needs to be refreshed?
What new things do we need to consider adding?

_____

Many churches do an overall review of their programs every few years. Here are questions that may help with such an assessment:

> Does this ministry continue to fit our church's
> mission and priorities?
> Does this ministry continue to serve its intended purpose?
> How can this ministry serve more effectively and efficiently?
> Is the cost in money and time proportionate
> with its fruitfulness?

———————————

Leaders regularly review monthly, quarterly, and annual reports. This method works well for assessing ongoing activities, but waiting for the end of a regular reporting period is not adequate for assessing new endeavors. New efforts require monitoring from the beginning with additional questions:

> What is the trajectory of the project?
> Is the initiative on a path to success or failure?

———————————

Portal ministries are those through which many new people enter your church. These entry points change over time. Dan Pezet suggests we ask these questions:

> What ministries have served as portal ministries for your church?
> How effective are they at connecting new people
> to your church today?

———————————

It is common to conduct an evaluation of an event or program. Research has shown that the most important number you need to know and compare across endeavors is the rating participants give to this question:

How likely is it that you would recommend this to a friend?

_____

Sometimes when goals are not reached, the mood is disappointment. A better stance is to see all results of our efforts as an opportunity to learn and improve, using questions such as these:

What did we learn?
What actions have we taken on the basis of what we learned?
What results have occurred from those actions?

ASSESSMENT QUESTIONS

Quickly learning from experiences is essential for leaders and groups. Margaret Wheatley shares four questions often used in an "After Action Review" by organizations and agencies:

What just happened?
Why do you think it happened?
What can we learn from this?
How will we apply these learnings?

_____

Leaders understand how important it is to ensure that efforts bear fruit. Vijay Govindarajan and Chris Trimble suggest that for any initiative, there are three modes of accountability needed, with each using a distinct question:

> Results—Did you achieve the predicted outcome?
> Actions—Did you execute the plan well?
> Learning—Did you follow a rigorous learning process?

———

A business journal ran an article with the subtitle, "Is the world better off because your company is in it?" Remembering it is "the world" that is the focus of God's love in the oft-quoted John 3:16, appropriate questions for us to ask are:

> Is the world better off because my church is in it?
> Is the world better off because I am in it?

———

Ozan Varol says that judging efforts only by whether they succeeded or failed is shortsighted. Good decisions can lead to failure just as bad practices can result in success. He suggests two questions to help with discernment following a failure:

> What went wrong with this failure?
> What went right with this failure?

———

Presbyterian pastor James Kim says it's one thing to have a mission and another to measure if ministries match the mission. His church's mission is "Make disciples and grow faithful disciples who share Christ's love with all people." All programs are measured by this mission using these questions about each:

> Is it making new disciples?
> Is it growing faithful disciples who obey God's commandments?
> Are these disciples sharing the love of Christ with all people?

Is your church so busy doing all its tasks that it is time to pause long enough to make sure your hard work is heading in the right and same direction? These questions may help you decide:

> Does everyone have a clear sense of the mission of the church?
> Do efforts and programs often feel unconnected
> with each other?
> Do teams feel disconnected from one another?
> Are the most active people feeling weary?
> Are you slow to adapt to changes in your context?

METRICS QUESTIONS

When beginning any new initiative, two questions to keep in mind are:

> What are the indicators we will monitor to determine
> if this effort is effective?
> Who will review the effectiveness of the initiative
> other than those who are leading it?

A fruitful exercise is to name as a group where you most hope God will lead your church in this next year. What will be different a year from now? What will increase? What will change? After doing this exercise, then you are ready to use this question to see how much attention these hopes are receiving:

What do we monitor regularly?

In an interview with Tony Morgan, Pastor Stephen DeFur of Cokesbury United Methodist Church in Knoxville, TN, tells about the questions his church asks, beyond attendance and financial issues, in order to monitor vitality. The questions include:

Are we connecting with unchurched people?
Are people taking next steps?
Are people professing their faith in Jesus?
Are people getting connected in small groups?
Are more people giving and serving others?

Baptist pastor David Hull tells how a right question by the Sunday School Director in his first church helped the pastor appreciate how important counting and paying attention to the results are. The church member asked this question:

In Jesus's parable about the lost sheep, how did the shepherd
know that one sheep was missing?

Usually when metrics come up in church discussions, the issues tend to revolve around numbers of people participating or dollars raised. Carey Nieuwhof suggests a more expansive way to use metrics that is focused on the people being served. He suggests these questions:

> Are people better off five years after joining your church
> than they were before?
> Do they feel closer to Christ?
> Are they making more of a difference in their workplaces
> and neighborhoods?

Reflections on Question Asking

Questions Address the Challenge of Competing Values

Good questions challenge your thinking. They reframe and redefine the problem. They throw cold water on our most dearly held assumptions and force us out of our traditional thinking. They motivate us to learn and discover more. They remind us of what is most important in our lives.

—Andrew Sobel and Jerold Panas[1]

In organizations there are always competing values and loyalties. People feel closest to those aspects of the mission with which they are involved or with which they identify most. These diverse values may not be equally essential to current priorities. However, if leaders devalue those more particular loyalties, people will not abandon them. In fact, if people sense that their values are challenged, they will cling more tightly to them. Leaders find ways to reframe issues in order to clarify the values and competing interests that always surround differing understandings of reality.

Generally, those interests and values are not bad, but they can be limiting if not put in some larger context. Without help, people will look at everything through the lens of their own values and immediate interests and can miss much else—instead of looking at their own interests in light of a larger vision. Effective leaders find ways to acknowledge those often-competing values in a way that permits people to see their own particular interests in light of a larger vision. So, the issues facing an organization can be reframed around larger values while not ignoring or devaluing those more particular interests.

Questions can provide a nonthreatening way to accomplish this task. For people attached to their own sphere of activities with little apparent interest beyond their work, there are questions that may be helpful. Questions that assume a key place for their particular work and ask their advice on how their work can contribute to larger goals may help them see their work as part of the larger mission. Or a leader may use questions that assume they already see their work not as an end in itself but as part of a larger mission. Follow up questions may explore how their contributions can be best optimized. Simply the act of engaging people who may feel disconnected from the mission beyond their specific tasks can be important to morale.

If the tasks of framing and reframing are not done in an active manner, then the leader is left always to respond to the different interests that are competing for priority. Without taking the initiative to put diverse goals into a larger vision, a leader will spend inordinate time trying to satisfy the various limited interests and resolve conflicts among competing claims without these efforts contributing necessarily to any larger aim.

Leading Change

Leadership is always about change. We cannot become what God calls us to be by remaining what we are. Nothing is more central to leading change than the discernment and realization of a compelling and shared appropriate vision. Leaders help God's people take their next faithful step. When hearing ideas for the future, leaders are often tempted to support those they like and resist those that do not appeal to them. Effective leaders come to see their task as helping themselves and others think clearly about various options. Support or opposition makes no sense until differing options are reviewed with probing questions. Then leaders help people navigate the change involved.

VISION QUESTIONS

When speaking to a group of church leaders, a panelist shared a question she uses to make sure new ideas connect to the purpose of the congregation. She responds to an idea with:

> That's a good idea. How does it fit with God's vision
> for our church?

Shawn Lovejoy suggests some splendid all-purpose questions for leaders to use regularly:

> Where are we going now?
> Where do we want to go?
> How do we take everyone there?

Church leadership is about change toward the next faithful step God has for us. Situations often seem complex, but three simple questions can keep a leader focused:

> What is the change or result we are seeking?
> How far along are we in reaching this goal?
> What do we need to do next to reach the goal?

Bishop Vashti Murphy McKenzie says leaders must know the destination they seek. One way she puts it is, "Where are you going?" Once clear on the destination, her suggested follow-up questions can help:

Does the journey require preparation?
Is there someone showing you the way?
Do you have everything you need for the journey?
Are there others riding with you, or are you going somewhere
by yourself?
Have you planned for detours or roadblocks?
What do you plan to do when you arrive?

A church wanted its vision to come alive within the congregation as a genuine guide for their ministry. When a proposed new initiative came up for discussion, this question helped the church stay focused on the vision:

Which part of our vision is this fulfilling?

INSPIRING CHANGE QUESTIONS

Leaders tell stories to help change take place. As they tell their change stories, leaders should keep in mind questions that are inevitably on their listeners' minds:

Where are we going?
Why is this change necessary?
What specific steps will need to be taken?
How can we make the change a success?
What's in it for us?

Church leaders often feel they are having to navigate a culture radically different from that in which they grew up. Old ways no longer seem to work. James Harnish poses a question that we might do well to raise in our congregations:

> What does it mean to be the body of Christ on this side
> of a cultural revolution?

Is your ministry changing to fulfill your mission in the new circumstances most churches face today? These questions suggest ways of assessing whether you truly have changed:

> Have our metrics changed?
> Do we count different things now?

Scott Cormode captures the dilemma of church leaders today in this perceptive question:

> How do you help people change who desperately need to change
> but desperately do not want to change?

Ronald Heifetz suggests that pacing the work of change leads to greater results. He offers questions to help leaders discern when issues are ready to be addressed:

> How stressful is the question or problem being raised,
> and how much loss does it involve?
> How resilient are the people being challenged?
> How strong are the bonds of authority that give one the power
> to hold people's attention to brutally hard questions?

ASSESSING DIFFERING DIRECTIONS QUESTIONS

Among the simplest and most overlooked questions for people facing a problem, challenge, or new opportunity are:

> How are others solving this problem?
> Addressing this challenge?
> Approaching this opportunity?

———————

Generating ideas from a group can be creative, but tension often occurs when choices have to be made among those suggestions. Minal Bopaiah suggests questions to help make such decisions:

> Which idea gets us closest to our desired outcome?
> Which idea is most likely to work for the people
> on whom we are concentrating?
> Which idea is most inclusive?

———————

When big decisions are made, there often comes a time for thoughtful appraisal before moving forward in a new direction. These questions may help:

> Will this effort solve the problem we have?
> If so, is this the best solution to the problem?
> And does it solve the problem without creating new problems?

———————

When undertaking an effort for which you have insufficient knowledge and experience, it is always a good idea to identify others who know more and talk with them. A good question to end each of those conversations is:

> Is there someone to whom you would go to learn more
> about this subject?

Churches wondering if a merger with another church might be best for their mission can consider these four questions offered by Jim Tomberlin and Warren Bird:

> Would our congregation be better by merging
> rather than remaining separate?
> Could we accomplish more together than we could separately?
> Would our community be better served if we joined together?
> Could the kingdom of God be further enlarged
> by joining together?

Harry F. Ward taught ethics at Union Theological Seminary in New York City in the first half of the twentieth century. A social activist, he was often provocative and controversial but also known for his careful attention to his teaching. In addressing many of the problems of his era, he encouraged students to engage three questions:

> What are the facts?
> What do they mean?
> What should be done?

DEALING WITH CHANGE QUESTIONS

In a liminal season, says Susan Beaumont, many of our old assumptions no longer hold true. Good questions can unfreeze some of our old assumptions and expand our consciousness:

> What was undervalued before that may hold greater value now?
> What mattered about geography before that no longer matters?
> What margin or lack of margin was built into our old model
> of doing church?
> What new abundance are we experiencing now?
> Where are we experiencing scarcity now that was not evident before?

Susan Beaumont says the journey through the pandemic has involved many painful losses including subtle but still painful losses associated with plans abandoned, dreams deferred, and the loss of control over our destiny. She suggests reflecting on these questions:

> What were we on the verge of discovering or accomplishing
> before the onset of the pandemic?
> What needs to move forward in different ways now?
> What was possible before that may not be possible
> for some time, if ever?
> What seemed important before that feels superfluous now?

Gil Rendle asks a provocative question that church leaders would do well to consider:

> What if the questions we now face are not the product of things
> gone wrong but rather of the world grown different?

———

Changing times and needs require churches to do things differently. Such change is a challenge for most churches. Perhaps these questions can help:

> Are there churches that seem to handle change especially well?
> What can we learn from them?
> When can we talk with them?

———

Alan Roxburgh offers a right question for churches seeking God's missional future:

> What are the challenges we currently face for which we presently
> have no answer but must address if we're to live into
> God's future for us?

Innovation

Good leaders are not wiser than other people. Rather, something that distinguishes good leaders from less effective leaders is their ability to challenge assumptions and to spot clues. One reason for that ability is that they are always paying attention. They notice the surprises and patterns that do not tend to follow conventional wisdom. Effective leaders also learn to cultivate their own creativity and to spark it in others. Great leaders do not necessarily have access to more information than others, but they learn to see in the ordinary the promise of new things. You and others do not have to create something new to see with new eyes the opportunities already present.

ASSUMPTIONS QUESTIONS

In 1993, Ellen Ochoa became the first Latina in space. Later, she moved into management at NASA around the time of the Space Shuttle *Challenger* disaster. Adam Grant reports she discovered that pride in performance often got in the way of asking hard questions. She developed questions to ask about every launch and major decisions:

> What leads you to that assumption?
> Why do you think it is correct?
> What might happen if it's wrong?
> What are the uncertainties in your analysis?
> I understand the advantages of your recommendation. What are the disadvantages?

A church that would normally extend a warm welcome to a new couple or family learned that a single, young adult had visited several times without anyone greeting or welcoming him. People did not seem to "know what to do" with a visitor who was different from their expectations.

> What assumptions or hidden biases may be limiting your church's mission?

Tod Bolsinger tells about the question asked of him after he had laid out an innovation initiative. It caused Tod to realize that whatever we propose must be focused more on the needs of others than on our own ideas. The question about his proposal was:

> Does it fix a real problem?

_____

Congregations often have a powerful sense of identity and a strong culture based on that identity. In such churches, a question often heard is, "Are we doing things our way?" Perhaps a better question could be:

> Is the way we are doing things bearing fruit?

_____

Any new endeavor involves a range of often unspoken assumptions. In addition to naming those assumptions so they can be tested, these two questions have been suggested:

> Which assumption, if wrong, would bring the entire initiative
> to an immediate halt?
> Is there any way to test this unknown first?

_____

Fernando F. Suarez and Juan S. Montes suggest that leaders question assumptions behind their organization's routines. Examples of helpful questions include:

> Where in the flow of work do problems consistently arise?
> Is there an argument for reshaping that segment
> or allocating more resources to it?
> What would happen if you suddenly had to get that chunk
> of work done much faster?

LOOKING FOR CLUES QUESTIONS

The Boston Red Sox baseball team in 1959 was the last to sign a Black player, twelve years after Jackie Robinson began playing for the Dodgers and three years after he retired. Through those years, Red Sox owner Tom Yawkey was told by his scouts that Black players were not ready for big league play despite ample evidence otherwise. Yawkey would have done well to ask two questions good leaders use:

> What may be missing in these reports?
> How do we verify the evaluations?

It is usually not a good idea to copy what another church is doing without considering your context. However, all of us can *learn* from what other congregations are doing. Wise church leaders regularly ask this question:

> What are churches just a bit larger than ours doing
> from which we can learn?

Pastors and other church leaders often have greater opportunities to know what is happening in churches other than their own. Given these opportunities, this can be a helpful question to ask from time to time:

> What innovations and initiatives that you see happening
> in churches like yours might you propose for consideration
> and discussion at your church?

Focus on one aspect of your church's ministry such as worship, children's ministry, youth ministry, etc., and ask these questions:

> What are the assumptions underlying what we are doing?
> Have they been tested recently?
> Have circumstances changed?

———

There are times to identify challenges, but it is also important to identify signs of life and hope in your congregation through questions such as these:

> What do you see already happening in our church
> that gives you the most hope for the future?
> What are we doing to build on this energy?

INSPIRING INNOVATION QUESTIONS

Rich Birch suggests questions that address issues most congregations are considering today:

> What will be the next normal?
> How will we transition into this next phase?
> What will change about our churches,
> and what will remain unchanged?
> How will we be changed as leaders because of all of this?

———

It's easy to dream too small or miss opportunities. Will Mancini tells about a meeting with church leaders in which a question sparked ideas leading to a new ministry in their community—one that had never come up for conversation before. He asked each person to respond to this question:

> What do you secretly believe your church would be great at
> but never told anyone?

———————

Churches rarely spend time debating bad ideas. The challenge is sorting through all the possible good things a church should do to discover just those few things that are right for your particular church and context at this moment. Questions to consider are:

> Does this strengthen and reinforce our core mission and values?
> Will it advance the next faithful step we believe God has
> for our church?
> Do we have the capacity to accomplish this
> without undercutting other ministries?
> Do the opportunities outweigh the challenges sufficiently
> to give a reasonable chance of success?

———————

Dwight Zscheile says in *The Agile Church* that innovation in the church requires asking tough questions, in safe environments, for which there are no easy answers. Some questions he suggests are:

> How do we share our faith with younger generations
> who don't seem interested?
> How can we form meaningful community with our neighbors
> in the name of Jesus?
> How can we give witness to abundant life in Christ
> in a broken world?
> What is God up to in our neighborhood?

———————

A time of focused conversations with different types of people within a relatively short timeframe can provide the makings of valuable insights about those you are seeking to reach. Imagine a small group of leaders finding ways to talk collectively with at least ten of the most active church members, ten of the least active, and ten people you are not now reaching. Usually there are those close enough to people in these three categories so that conversations would not be awkward. The conversations do not have to be especially about the church but about their lives as a whole—hopes, concerns, and interests. Then, the small group of interviewers can come together to talk about similarities and differences among the groups using questions such as:

> What do they all have in common?
> What are the differences?
> What do the similarities and differences suggest that would help
> our church serve them all better?

Most change is modest and incremental. This kind of change is good, but occasionally it may be wise to test the limits of our creativity by asking bold questions that force everyone to move beyond their zone of comfort and conventional thinking. Who knows what never-thought-of-before idea might emerge when you pick a question such as:

> What would we do differently if our church makeup
> had to match that of the community in three years?
> What might we do if we had to double our income in one year?
> How would we do things if we had to reduce expenses
> by 50 percent?

ENCOURAGING CREATIVITY QUESTIONS

Churches often take on the most common practices of other churches in their community and region. This is especially the case when one denomination or theological tradition tends to overwhelm others in numbers and influence. In such cases, a good question for your church might be:

> What might it mean to "go opposite" some of the dominant
> practices to offer fresh alternatives?

Michael Frost and Alan Hirsch suggest a way to break open thinking about church:

> What would your experience of church be like:
> a) if you no longer had a building?
> b) if you could no longer meet on Sundays?
> c) if you had no pastor or clearly identifiable leadership team?

Discussions about what to do next in a ministry area often sound much like previous conversations. A way of changing the dynamic is to ask the group (or, even better, divide and use multiple groups) to pretend that they are consultants engaged by the congregation to do an analysis of the ministry topic at hand. They are to prepare a response to this question:

> Given what you have learned about our church, what are
> your most objective observations and what are your best
> recommendations for next steps our church might take?

Often churches must picture a stronger future in their minds before they can take steps to make it a reality. One church asks its leaders to close their eyes and picture their church five or ten years from now if it were fulfilling God's will for them in their community. Then they use questions such as these:

> Whom do you see in the pews at worship?
> Who is walking through the hallways?
> What is going on during the week?
> What is happening in the evenings?

———————

In a presentation before a group of clergy and laity, Professor Kenda Creasy Dean asked this question:

> How has your church become more curious in the past year?

———————

Saj-nicole A. Joni helps leaders think more broadly about their work through questions such as:

> How diverse is my inner circle?
> Am I pushing inquiry to the limits regularly?
> Who really makes me think in new ways?

Reflections on Question Asking

Questions Lead to Discoveries

Have you noticed that in the Gospels Jesus asks a ton of questions? In every situation, he's asking questions. I think Jesus may have asked even more questions than Socrates ever did.

—Martin B. Copenhaver[1]

When facing adaptive challenges for which the problem or solution or both are unknown, Ronald Heifetz reminds leaders that the crucial step is not to do something but rather to ask, "What do we need to learn?" It is a good reminder that the power of leaders comes from relationships and constant learning. Questions give an opportunity to let people know that you do not have all the answers and that you need their help to learn what you do not know. Others will respond not by thinking less of you but more. Your willingness to ask for their knowledge builds a stronger bond than would be the case otherwise.

Curiosity and questioning are essential for innovation and creativity. Questions open the mind to new possibilities. They acknowledge the need for insights beyond your own. Questions present new occasions for discoveries every time they are asked. That is why open-ended questions are the gold standard for questioning. Such questions give others maximum opportunity to draw from their experience to contribute to expanding the knowledge needed for next steps.

The Trappist monk Thomas Merton tells of his extraordinary experience of having Mark Van Dorn as a teacher at Columbia University. While Van Dorn had much knowledge to teach, most of the time he asked questions, according to Merton. "His questions were good, and if you tried to answer them intelligently, you found yourself saying excellent things that you did not know you knew, and that you had not, in fact, known before," Merton recalls. Van Dorn "educed" these creative responses from his students that Merton explains this way:

> What he did have was the gift of communicating to them something of his own vital interest in things, something of his manner of approach: but the results were sometimes quite unexpected—and by that I mean good in a way that he had not anticipated, casting lights that he had not himself foreseen.[2]

Expanding Reach and Impact

Each year many congregations withdraw the scope of their witness within their communities instead of expanding their reach and impact. But churches thrive through ongoing renewal and revitalization. Not only is a congregation called to serve its current members but also to be an inviting place where others begin and continue their faith journeys. Christians have a passion for others to know the love of God, and churches that lose this evangelical spirit suffer. Churches that find respectful and sensitive ways to convey God's love revealed in Christ to those outside their faith community thrive. Today those most missing from congregations are those younger than current participants and those different from present members racially or economically.

REVITALIZATION QUESTIONS

If an organization remains too protective of the status quo, it can impede significant adaptive change, says Susan Beaumont. She suggests that these questions can invite innovation:

What is our greatest asset now?
What relationships will we need to build on or strengthen
in the months ahead?
What unique role might our congregation play in local, national,
and even global recovery?
What long-term changes in the bigger picture would we
like to be part of bringing to fruition?

In reflecting on the contemporary meaning of the Protestant Reformation, ethicist Margaret A. Farley challenges us to look for reforms that are needed today. She offers questions to help:

Where is the injury and what are its causes?
Where is the apathy and what can awaken us?
Where are the old and the new springs of life,
and how shall they be released?

Traditions can be good so long as they do not become barriers to what God wants us to do next. Tony Morgan suggests two questions to ask about traditions:

Is it sacred or is it familiar?
Is it holy or is it comfortable?

Alan Hirsch uses two questions with churches seeking to revitalize their ministries:

> If you could start all over again, would you do it the same way?
> If not, why are you doing it the same way now?

Clif Christopher, an expert on improving financial stewardship, says that often what appears to be a money problem may have to do with other things. He offers three questions when churches think they have financial problems:

> Are you sure your problem is money?
> How good is your worship?
> How united is your staff?

REACHING NEW DISCIPLES QUESTIONS

Dan Pezet offers questions to help you discover the most vital entry points for your congregation. Think of your newest members, and then ask:

> How did they connect?
> What was the first ministry in which they participated?

Churches are normally aware of groups of people in their communities who are not present in their congregations. While churches wish their constituencies were more reflective of their communities, little may change without specific steps. Roman Catholic priest Michael White suggests three questions that should help, once we identify those not present:

> What, specifically, are you going to do about it?
> Who is doing it?
> How are you keeping track of how well you're doing?

The day-to-day functions of a congregation can easily absorb the energies of all leaders until some of the basic tasks required by the church's mission are neglected. Rich Birch offers a good reminder about one of these essential efforts and suggests this question:

> Which leaders in your church are responsible for new people coming to your church next Sunday?

Leaders need a right question to use when proposals aimed at reaching new people are rejected. For example, in a congregation with declining attendance, "dinner church" was suggested as a way to reach new people in their growing community. Church leaders said "no" to the idea. The person who made the proposal said, "OK. But I know the new people around our church are on your heart as much as they are on mine." Then came the question:

> If dinner church doesn't work for you, tell me what comparable innovation God has put on your hearts that might accomplish the same goal of reaching people for Christ?

In his book on evangelism, *New Wine, New Wineskins: How African American Congregations Can Reach New Generations*, Doug Powe suggests that churches seeking to reach new people ask themselves these questions:

> Are you merely a drive-in-for-Sunday-service-and-Bible-study congregation?
> Is your congregation willing to create a space for those who are truly seeking a relationship with God?
> How consistent is your witness in the community?

Historian James Hudnut-Beumler writes insightfully about both the history and future of mainline Protestantism. He features a simple but essential question that applies to all congregations. He says that the "whither mainline Protestantism" dilemma hangs on an answer to this question:

> How do mainline Protestants recruit or bring in new members?

REACHING YOUNGER PEOPLE QUESTIONS

Many churches seek to reach younger people, and some may be giving younger people ministry responsibility before they are "ready." Rich Birch reminds current "older" church leaders that they may have become who they are because they were trusted with ministry responsibility before they were "ready." And he asks this blunt question:

> Who are the young leaders that you are irrationally trusting
> to lead parts of the ministry?

Carey Nieuwhof, a Canadian pastor and popular blogger, has many ask him about reaching unchurched people because of his success in doing just that in his church. He has a theory about what it takes to reach the unchurched: He believes that if teens find your main worship services boring, irrelevant, and disengaging, so will unchurched people. He says that if you can design services that engage teenagers, you have designed a service that engages unchurched people. Therefore, his right question for churches is:

> Do the teens in your church love your services
> and want to invite their friends?

Have you noticed when walking through a house, you can often tell when it was built or last updated? So it is with churches. Carey Nieuwhof says that "every church has a date on it" and then provides a right question your church may want to ask:

> What is the date on your church?

Those interested in connecting more with young people can utilize a question offered by David Olshine. He suggests a congregational leader treat some of the teenagers to lunch and conversation. There is one question in which the leader's role is to listen closely, take notes, make no comments, and express thanks. His recommended question:

> From your point of view, what should church look like?

Research by the Fuller Youth Institute suggests that realistic role models help young people develop faith and character. In *Faith Beyond Youth Group*, they suggest questions to help young people identify who has modeled character growth for them. These include:

> Which teachers, coaches, or other adults do you admire most
> and why?
> Which peers do you admire and look up to
> for how they live their lives?
> How have your parents modeled growth to you?
> They follow with questions that help youth reflect
> on the significance and meaning of these models.

REACHING UNDERREPRESENTED CONSTITUENCIES QUESTIONS

Churches often have an image of what new members might look like. Chances are that churches similar to yours are seeking those same people. Try using this question to spark new ideas:

> Who are the people in our community that all churches
> are overlooking?

_____

Rick Rusaw and Brian Mavis encourage the concept of being a "neighboring church" by asking their church members these questions about their nearest neighbors:

> How many names do you know?
> Do you know something about each of them?
> Can you tell some hurt or hope or dream they have?

_____

Often after tragedies in which many are killed, including from natural disasters, there will be reports coming long after the event about how many bodies of victims have not yet been claimed. A question that might bring this closer to home is to ask these questions:

> Who are the people in our community who, if they died,
> might have no one to claim their bodies?
> Do we know their names?
> Do we have any connection with them?

_____

Often churches know and also regret that they are not reaching some of the most marginal and vulnerable people in their communities. To help address this concern, one congregation asks:

> Who are the people in our community that no one else wants,
> and how can we love them the way God loves them?

How do we look at newcomers? What questions do we ask about them and ourselves? Molly Phinney Baskette reports how important a few right questions were in helping her small congregation become the church home for many new people. They asked:

> How does God want us to be church for them,
> and how can we open our doors even wider?
> What do they have to offer and teach us—
> and how can we make their gifts visible?
> How can we honor their presence among us?

Church Ministries

Churches implement their mission through a range of ministries throughout the year. Each of these ministries has its own purposes that flow into the overall congregational mission. These ministries need sustaining innovation that comes from incremental improvements and constant focus on whether they are fulfilling their purposes in the best ways possible. Effective leaders seek to improve these ongoing ministries even as they explore new arenas for ministry.

CHILDREN QUESTIONS

Lee Kricher tells about an important moment for his church when they realized they were working from an unspoken assumption: "If it was good enough for me, it is good enough for our children." They discovered that nothing changed until they went from an unspoken assumption to a stated question:

> What will it take to reach our children?

————————

Lee Kricher also asks:

> Which of these statements would people be most likely
> to hear you say?
> (1) "If it was good enough for me, it will be good enough
> for our children."
> Or (2) "Let's do whatever it takes to reach the next generation."

————————

Gil Rendle suggests that when older church members with grandchildren are upset about some of the new music used in worship, the following may help:

> Would you sacrifice a great deal for your grandchildren?
> Would you be willing to learn a new kind of music so your
> grandchildren would be involved in church?

————————

Bill Tenny-Brittian reminds us that a question churches should ask is one near to the hearts of any parents with young children:

> Does your nursery get an A+ in the three S's
> (Sanitation, Safety, and Security)?

DISCIPLESHIP QUESTIONS

John M. Perkins is concerned with the cultural captivity of the church in which "we aren't calling people to much of anything." He follows with a provocative question:

> What kind of commitment is required for you to join the
> congregation you are part of?

In thinking about increasing generosity among members, Rosario Picardo suggests we keep in mind things potential givers want to know.

> Does my giving make a difference?
> Do I matter to my faith community?
> How will my resources be used?
> What is the vision I'm giving toward,
> and what is the plan for reaching it?
> How can I get involved in the ministry
> I am supporting financially?

Will Willimon speaks in a sermon about the rich man who goes on a journey and entrusts his property to workers, giving one five talents, another two talents, and the third, one talent (Matthew 25:14ff.). Upon the rich man's return, the workers faced the same question, Willimon reminds us, that all of us face:

> What have you done with what you were given?

An acquaintance said to pastor Rick Rusaw, "When I first became a Christian, I had a really small house but a really big heart. Now I have a really big house but a really small heart. I want a bigger heart." The question that led to this acknowledgement was:

> How has your heart grown in the past twelve months?

Church leaders constantly want to involve new people, and yet the same people end up doing most things. It could be that our tendency when a need arises is to turn to those with whom there is a close connection and who are willing workers. Nelson Searcy suggests a question that can regularly open many doors through which new people might enter to serve:

> What are we doing this week that could get more people
> involved in serving than last week?

In noting Matthew 6:21, "Where your treasure is, there your heart will be also," Jacob Armstrong suggests two questions:

> Where do I *want* to invest my treasure?
> Where am I *really* investing my treasure?

MISSION AND OUTREACH QUESTIONS

The *Alban Weekly* newsletter shared good questions for church leaders to consider as they assess their congregational and community needs:

What challenges does your congregation or community face
that cannot be addressed with money alone?
How might your programs or outreach change if they were done
with people instead of for people?
What risks is your congregation willing to take
for the sake of your neighbors?
With whom can you partner in meeting the needs
of your neighbors?

The Resourceful Communities program of The Conservation Fund suggests seven questions congregations should ask when considering a community ministry:

1. What resources does your church have to engage
in a ministry project?
2. What do you know about your community that has inspired
this ministry idea, and what more do you need to know?
3. Who are you partnering with in this ministry?
4. Who will primarily benefit from your ministry?
5. How can those who will benefit be a part
of the planning process?
6. How do you know that people will utilize and benefit
from your ministry?
7. What specific need is your ministry addressing?

F. Douglas Powe, in writing about how one group of congregations can connect with their communities and better reach new generations, asked a question appropriate for all churches:

> How do churches become missional and not simply
> congregations with a mission?

_____

Churches are increasingly investing themselves in service to their communities. Facing the major decision of where and how they can make the most difference for the people in the community, one church uses this question:

> What is needed in our community that no one else is doing?

SPIRITUAL LIFE QUESTIONS

In their book *8 Virtues of Rapidly Growing Churches*, Matt Miofsky and Jason Byassee suggest that the right question is not "When were you saved?" but rather:

> How are you growing in grace just now?

_____

Theologian Gordon Kaufman said that the most essential questions for theology are not primarily speculative but more practical. Two such questions he suggested are:

> How are we to live?
> To what should we devote ourselves?

_____

John Wesley had a few simple questions for those prospective leaders of the early Methodist movement:

> Have they faith?
> Have they gifts?
> Have they fruit?

All Christian leaders face the challenge of continuing their spiritual discipleship pilgrimage amid all the challenges of the moment. One pastor reports that she seeks to stay accountable by asking God these three questions each day:

> How may I glorify you?
> How might I point others to Christ?
> (And at the end of the day) Did I love today?

Tod Bolsinger tells of two friends and mentors who used email and even postcards occasionally to ask questions that kept him spiritually grounded. Each always began with "I am praying for you." Then came a question such as these two:

> What are you doing for God's kingdom today?
> How are you feeling about glorifying God in your life?

Finding ways to experience renewal is always a challenge for leaders. Even religious leaders often find Sabbath experiences missing in their lives.

Someone who has spent many years on committees interviewing candidates for positions has found these questions helpful:

> If you had an entire day to do just what you wanted to do,
> how would you spend the day?
> How long has it been since you spent a day like that?

STEWARDSHIP AND FINANCE QUESTIONS

Erin Weber-Johnson suggests that contextual factors are critical to understanding why and how people give. She offers questions to use with church members to learn more of the stewardship culture of your congregation. Her questions include:

> What are your earliest experiences of giving?
> Why have you given in the past?
> When have you felt most inspired to give?
> What would make it easier to give?
> How would you like to be asked?

———————

Trevor Dancer, while pastor of Central United Methodist Church in Kansas City, Missouri, asked his congregation this question in a sermon on stewardship:

> If people knew how much you give, would they be inspired to
> give more themselves?

Mike Slaughter, in his book *The Christian Wallet: Spending, Giving, and Living with a Conscience,* proposes three right questions to ask each time we prepare to spend money:

> Why am I spending?
> Whose money is it that I am spending?
> What are God's priorities in my spending?

———

Any church leader responsible for stewardship seeks ways to communicate about money that will connect with others and their faith commitments, while also understanding the anxiety the subject tends to elicit. Margaret Marcuson suggests that a helpful beginning point is to understand better what *you* think about giving. Such clarity may help you understand the range of thinking and feeling others bring to the subject. Her suggested questions are:

> Why do you give?
> What did you learn about giving from your family of origin?
> Why do you give the amount you give?
> Why do you give where you give?

———

Howard Stevenson suggests questions donors must implicitly say "yes" to when deciding to support a cause:

> Are you doing important work?
> Are you well managed?
> Will my gift make a difference?
> Will the experience be satisfying to me?

———

Leaders set the tone for a congregation's culture. Whether leaders are paid or volunteer, their words convey values picked up by others. Sometimes leaders with good intentions send messages inconsistent with the direction the church is seeking to go. This can send mixed messages, and worse, it supports a mindset at odds with the church at its best. This may happen when people repeat language they heard growing up in church. For example, the faithful finance chair makes the case for financial support using language of guilt and obligation at odds with the theology of stewardship the church seeks to build. A question that can help address this problem and educate as well is:

> What are the "we must never use" phrases for our church?

WORSHIP QUESTIONS

Charlie Baber notes that worship is often planned primarily from the perspective of those already attending church. He suggests questions that might help shape worship with a broader mission:

> What sort of worship reaches those people in your town who
> most need the power of God's love in Christ?
> How is your music inspiring people to a deeper community
> and deeper faith?
> How is your worship grounded in the faith of the past, while
> evolving with the people God has placed in your community?

———————

Co-pastors of a church designing Christmas Eve worship in the midst of the COVID-19 pandemic first asked members of their Worship Committee to name what had been most meaningful to them about Christmas Eve worship in the past. Recognizing that many traditions would not be possible this year, they changed the tone of the conversation in a way that created genuine excitement. They asked:

> What can we do this year that will be so memorable that people will be talking about it for decades to come?

The language we use in church is so familiar to most of us that we seldom think that our words may not communicate clearly to those new to the church. A pastor recently used a question at the end of the worship service to great benefit:

> Was there any word in today's bulletin
> that you did not understand?
> Worshipers were asked to circle such words on their bulletins
> and leave them at a designated place as they departed.

Michael White and Tom Corcoran suggest the following questions about music in a congregation.

> Would we say we have a *music* program or a *worship* program?
> Is our music the personal preference of the pastor, music
> director, parish? OR is our music about attracting the lost and
> growing disciples through worship?
> On a scale of 1 to 10, how much participation is there
> in our music program on the weekends?

While acknowledging that effective preaching styles vary, one writer suggests four characteristics of preaching that are often found in vital congregations. Phrased as questions, they are:

> Is it biblical?
> Is it joyful?
> Is it life-related?
> Is it invitational?

Reflections on Question Asking

Use Questions for Insight and Not for Blame

We do not grow by knowing all of the answers,
but rather by living with the questions.

—Max De Pree[1]

Good leaders live in a world in which results matter, as they should. A vital part of a leader's calling is to keep everyone focused on the mission and to achieve the goals of that mission. For most in any organization, talk of results brings anxiety about judgment that may be coming their way for goals missed. That may happen, of course, but leaders need to be careful not to communicate judgment as a primary purpose. The reason to draw attention to goals and results is that only then can you help shape planning needed to accomplish the goals.

Leaders depend on asking questions that report how things are going, but the "meeting or missing goals" is not the true purpose of these questions. The results reported may show goals reached, but they are just as likely to show missed goals. The real benefit of using questions to discuss results comes from what is *learned* from the results. Apparent "failure" may be the beginning of positive results if failure can produce important insights for changes.

Coworkers should know that they need not fear judgment but can take the opportunity to identify what was learned, identify changes to make from those learnings, and illustrate that progress can be made. Whenever there are questions that elicit objective results, always include questions that give a chance for narratives and insights. The focus is on learning, not judging.

Community Concerns

Churches that grow and make an impact on their communities give attention beyond the walls of their congregations. These churches are known as "good churches" even by those who belong to other churches or have no faith themselves. People know and appreciate churches with strong community ties that seek the best for all in the community. These churches are especially attuned to ways they can contribute to more inclusive and just communities in which all are valued and participate.

CONNECTING WITH YOUR COMMUNITY QUESTIONS

Some churches know their neighbors well. Others do not. G. Travis Norvell suggests a place to begin in determining how well you know your neighbors by using these questions:

> Do you know the names of the neighbors who border
> your church's property?
> Who are they?
> How long have they lived there?
> What do they think of the church?

———————

Church leaders frequently encourage spiritual discernment for themselves and other individuals when faced with important decisions. Such discernment is also needed for congregations as they examine their circumstances and context through the eyes of their mission. One question suggested for such congregational discernment is:

Where is God drawing us as a community?

George Thompson offers these two questions to help your church stay attuned to changing circumstances:

What is beginning to change in your community?
How are you responding?

Pastor G. Travis Norvell encourages churches to "draw your parish" as a way of understanding better the community your church serves. After thinking of the boundaries that make sense for your parish, he suggests you ask these questions:

Who calls it home?
What brings joy to those who call it home?
What causes pain in the parish?
Where is God already at work in your parish?

Luke Edwards offers questions church leaders can use when they seek to "listen" to their communities and better understand their context and neighbors:

> What do my neighbors care about?
> Where do my neighbors gather?
> What burdens do my neighbors carry?
> Who in my community is disconnected from church
> in its current form?

Dave Harder says that the church lives in a connected world yet often with limited connections. He proposes a question to help the situation:

> Could we imagine the answers that will propel us into a vibrant and flourishing future are not going to be found inside a church building but on the sidewalks, in coffee shops, and on front porches in our neighborhoods?

DIVERSITY QUESTIONS

Adam Grant tells about Daryl Davis, who played piano at many country music venues. Often, he was the only Black person present, and sometimes was among people with racial prejudice. When things got tense in those situations, Daryl used a question he remembers using the first time he experienced overt racism. When he was ten years old and marching in a Cub Scout parade, white spectators started throwing things at the kids. His question:

> How can you hate me when you don't even know me?

Alicia Garza, co-organizer of Black Lives Matter, uses a distinctive approach in countering stereotypical comments associated with certain racial or ethnic groups, such as why so many people live in the same house or why working age adults are standing around during the workday. She responds with questions of her own, such as:

> I've seen that too. What do you think it's like to live in a house with so many people? or
> I saw that too. Why are so many Black people, particularly Black men, unemployed?

Pastor Kevin Murriel suggests two questions that he finds helpful when people want to have open conversations about race:

> Where did I first learn about race?
> Who influences my perspective on race today?

Robin Diangelo writes and consults about issues of racial and social justice. In sessions she leads, an exercise she uses is to ask people in clusters of three to take one minute each to answer this question:

> What are some of the ways in which your race has shaped your life?

Ella F. Washington is an organizational psychologist who helps groups make progress on diversity, equity, and inclusion. Questions she suggests include:

Why does diversity and inclusion matter to us personally?
Where do we want to go?
How can diversity help us to meet our other goals?
What's our strategy?

———————

A church wanting to reach a broader constituency in their community asked these questions:

What kind of people tend to come to our church?
What kind of people tend not to come to our church?
Why do you think this is the case?

JUSTICE QUESTIONS

Dr. Jacqueline Lewis encourages parents to teach their children "fierce love." She suggests these questions:

Who will you choose to teach your children *to be*?
What will you teach them about what is loving, just, and fair?

———————

Leslie Dunbar, ally of key civil rights leaders, tells of a time when Martin Luther King, Jr., faced criticism for his opposition to the Vietnam War, including participation in an antiwar march. The next day King and other civil rights leaders were together. Another well-known civil rights leader said to King, "Martin, I see you were marching yesterday." King replied with what Dunbar calls "the prophet's question":

"Yes, I was. And where were you?"

———————

Robert D. Putnam has written incisive and provocative books that help interpret changes in society. In one focused specifically on religion, *American Grace: How Religion Divides and Unites Us*, he includes this pivotal question for the nation's future:

> How can religious pluralism coexist with religious polarization?

Courtney E. Martin, in writing about her decision regarding where to enroll her young daughter in school, cites a question paraphrased from Nikole Hannah-Jones:

> If a school isn't good enough for your kid,
> why is it good enough for any kid?

In working toward greater diversity and equity, leaders may use questions for group discussion to help surface unspoken assumptions affecting participants' attitudes and actions. Examples used in one inclusion instrument are:

> What messages did I receive when I was growing up
> about different races and ethnicities?
> What messages did I receive about other dimensions of diversity?
> How might these messages be influencing how I see the world?

Michael R. Fisher offers questions for congregations wanting to be positive contributors to the justice issues all communities face:

> What actions has our congregation taken to address
> racial inequality in our community?
> How have we used our congregation's resources to support
> racial injustices or support racial justice?
> What do these answers mean then for how we are going
> to live out our faith in the future?

IMPACT ON SOCIETY QUESTIONS

Robert D. Putnam asked this question of religion in general, but the question may be appropriate for a congregation. Perhaps you want to add some other societal changes to those he names.

> How has religion engaged three major trends in American
> society: the revolution in women's rights, rising income
> inequality, and growing ethnic and racial diversity?

John Perkins's work in racial reconciliation and justice over a lifetime leads him to believe church leaders in white churches mistakenly believe that if people believe right, they will act right. He offers this question for consideration:

> How are you helping your church learn to love?

Columnist and evangelical Christian Michael Gerson in discussing a recent denominational controversy reminded us that "during every generation across two millennia, Christians have faced the question":

> Do they oppose and confront the worst elements
> of their culture, or do they reflect and amplify them?

——————————

Laity in one congregation were preparing sack lunches for children during the summer months—needed due to the absence of school lunches. One layperson captured the necessary link between deeds of mercy and justice by asking this question:

> What more can we do so that the time will come
> when no one must provide sack lunches?

——————————

Michael R. Fisher suggests that congregations cannot address justice issues in their communities alone. He offers these questions to consider.

> With whom can we partner?
> With whom are we in regular dialogue to increase our witness
> as a congregation that stands for justice?

——————————

Ethicist Robert Franklin, while president of Morehouse College, speculated about what it would mean for colleges to receive "community accreditation" to go along with all the other types of accreditations required of them. It's an interesting idea not just for colleges but also for churches and each of us. What would it be like for us and our congregations to answer regularly questions such as:

> What does the community think of the performance
> and value of your work?
> What have you done in the past year
> to enhance the community?
> How could you become a better citizen of your community?

Personnel

Few decisions are more critical to the future of any organization than those involving the selection of personnel. A strong, gifted, growing, and trained cadre of leaders is essential for ongoing church vitality. In some organizations, such staffing and hiring decisions come infrequently enough that a foundation of best practices may not be in place.

STAFFING AND HIRING QUESTIONS

When assessing the performance of new personnel, there are usually some obvious results of their work that can be gathered. However, a better question in those early months may be:

> What is their ability to learn, grow, and adjust?

Peter Drucker maintained that the most important decisions in organizations are people decisions, but we rarely evaluate how we are doing on these selections. He suggests using this question with each hire, reviewing it three years later to see if it worked out, and keeping a score of how well you are doing:

> If we put this person in this position, what do we expect him or
> her to accomplish?

Consultant Susan Beaumont says that churches often develop personnel planning and funding based on current practice. She offers questions churches could ask to think more carefully about personnel and mission:

> What staffing changes are required to support
> our current strategic priorities?
> Are we being just and fair in how we pay our employees?
> Does our investment in payroll *support* or *diminish*
> the ministry of our laity?

A question asked in many congregations fairly regularly is "What percentage of the church's budget is for staff?" It certainly never hurts to know this number and how it compares with truly comparable churches. However, Florida United Methodist pastor Steve Price finds that a "one size fits all" approach to such percentages is not always helpful. He proposes that a better question might be:

> What kind of correlation do we see between our investment
> in staff and the impact the church is having on members,
> the community, and the world?

WORKING WITH STAFF QUESTIONS

Reviews, whether for staff or volunteers, tend to be crowded out by other things, especially those that come outside any required annual reviews. Increasingly churches are finding that building in some "along the way" conversations, ideally quarterly, helps everyone. Questions sometimes used are:

> What recent success has meant much to you?
> What is your most important goal in the coming months?
> What do you need in order to achieve that goal?

The principal of a school was viewed as quite rigid and unapproachable. His supervisor, after affirming many aspects of the principal's work, shared the negative perceptions held by the coworkers. A few months later, the complaints had ended. The principal had begun meeting with the staff monthly to ask two questions and then listen carefully. His questions were:

> How are you doing?
> What can I do to help?

The Bible is filled with wonderful questions, but "Who is to be regarded as greatest among us?" is not one of them. For those serving in the church as lay and ordained leaders, perhaps these three questions better help us move toward the fulfillment of God's purpose for the church and for all of our lives:

> The question of calling:
> What is your particular calling from God?
> The question of support:
> Do you have what you need to fulfill your calling?
> The question of accountability:
> Are you fulfilling your calling?

Someone involved in intentional interim ministry reports that she learned the "RAA" questions to ask oneself about a situation:

> Who is Responsible?
> Have they been given the Authority?
> To whom are they Accountable?

Deborah Ike has offered six right questions that leaders can ask of church staff:

> What can I do to help?
> If you could do any job, even somewhere else,
> what would it be and why?
> How can I improve as a leader?
> What's an issue that needs attention but I haven't noticed, and
> how would you address it?
> How does your family feel about church?
> Do they feel part of it or jealous of it?

EVALUATING STAFF QUESTIONS

If you supervise others and have year-end review sessions coming up, you might consider these questions one supervisor used last year that led to positive results:

> What are you proud of accomplishing this year?
> What are your goals for the coming year?
> How can I support you in achieving those goals?

Year-end staff reviews are common in churches, but what about doing a year-end congregation review?! If you are daring enough to give this a try, you may want to consider some questions secular organizations use to track how they are doing from one year to another. All questions need ranking options with them.

> How satisfied are you with the overall ministry
> of [church name]?
> How likely are you to continue your participation
> in [church name]?

> If you were choosing a church for the first time, how likely
> would you be to choose [church name]?
> How strongly do you feel that [church name]
> sets an example of excellence?
> How likely are you to recommend [church name]
> to someone else?

In the secular workplace, "derailment" is a term often used in relation to new leaders who do not work out. There are some common characteristics associated with those who derail. Here are a few questions to help assess if someone may be a candidate for derailment:

> Am I always right and everyone else is wrong?
> Do I grab the center of attention?
> Do I let my mood swings affect my leadership?
> Do I focus on negatives?
> Do I get little things right but the big things wrong?

Dave Ulrich believes that effective leaders combine personal credibility and organizational capability or "credibility x capability." Examples of questions for each include:

> Do individuals trust, respect, admire, and enjoy working
> with this leader?
> Can this leader shape a vision, create commitment to the vision,
> build a plan of execution, develop capabilities, and hold people
> accountable for making things happen?

Two questions leaders in one church have used during annual staff reviews are:

> On what do you wish you could spend more time?
> On what are you now spending time or too much time
> without proportionate results?

SUPPORTING LEADERS QUESTIONS

To provide effective support for staff and volunteer leaders, it is helpful to ask:

> What are the stumbling blocks that make it more difficult
> for you to accomplish your work?

———

Persons may well benefit from networking with others who have similar responsibilities and goals. A leader might ask:

> How can I facilitate connections between highly motivated staff
> and volunteers with those doing similar work in other settings?

———

When ideas emerge in congregations, Robert Schnase suggests that asking to which committee this idea should be taken may not be the best first question. He suggests another question:

> Who are the other people who share this interest, passion,
> and calling, and how do we connect with them?

———

Staff report that they meet too infrequently with their supervisors, and when they do, the topics tend to be those chosen by the supervisor. Here are questions from which supervisors might draw in such meetings to connect better with their staff:

What are things on your mind for us to address first?
What are your current priorities, and how can I help?
What do I need to know about your work
so I can support you well?

Dave Ferguson and Warren Bird focus on the way Jesus and Paul developed other leaders by using the concept of "hero making." The right question they suggest for leaders is:

Am I trying to be the hero, or am I trying to make heroes
out of others?

Reflections on Question Asking

Ways to Enhance Your Question Asking

Asking good questions can be a weirdly vulnerable activity.
You're admitting that you don't know.

—David Brooks[1]

MAKE SURE YOU LISTEN WELL

When you ask questions, you have already sent a message that you are willing to listen. Be sure not to undercut that advantage by not paying close attention. You are listening for content that can be captured in notes, but you are listening much more for nuance. Important signals may come from the emotions of speakers or their apathy. Pay attention to who speaks and those that do not. And especially listen for what is not being said. For example, if the conversation is about values, you may notice that a supposed core value of the organization never comes up.

LEARN TO USE ALTERNATIVE QUESTIONS

If questioning becomes a part of how you lead, you will need to become adept at asking the same thing in numerous ways—not just for variety but with a different nuance that draws different responses. You will notice in the questions shared in this volume there are familiar patterns that are adjusted to fit a different context or topic. These templates will become helpful to you as you move among various constituencies and responsibilities. A different type of alternative question occurs when you discover the need for a substitute or replacement question. A question you anticipate will draw prompt response from others may fall flat. In those cases, be ready to pivot to another line of questioning.

HAVE FOLLOW UP QUESTIONS READY
WHEN NEEDED

There are some occasions when a follow up question or questions may be useful. You never want to move too quickly to follow up questions, lest you miss the fullness of the original contributions. Even when you have follow up questions planned, pay attention to the dynamics of the discussion and feel free to abandon the extra questions or change them based on the flow of contributions. You do not want to do anything to dampen energy that is evident or to probe something for which the group appears not ready to engage.

Management Skills

Good management skills normally come from a mixture of training, experience, and paying attention to how others do things. Management may not be the most glamorous activities for leaders, but such tasks are essential. We learn just how important good management is when it is absent. The greatest of dreams will falter unless leaders pay attention to basic management skills.

COMMUNICATION QUESTIONS

Communication is one of the primary ways that people lead. Dianna Booher provides questions all leaders would do well to ask about their communication. Among them are:

> Is your communication correct?
> Is your communication complete?
> Is your communication clear?
> Is your communication consistent?

Some churches today recognize that they must move to the next chapter in their history since as good as the past chapter has been, it no longer fits today's context. In such situations, wise advice for leaders is captured in this simple question:

> How do you communicate your new identity
> while respecting your past one?

A consultant felt good about how he had helped a leader develop the best way to make an important presentation to his constituents. To the consultant's surprise, the speech did not go well. The consultant realized he had asked many questions about the content of the presentation but failed to ask this important question:

> How do you think those hearing this presentation
> will respond to it?

Two questions are useful for preachers and speakers as they plan a presentation to a group:

> What is going on in the lives of the people hearing my message
> to which I can connect my presentation?
> What is going on in the community, nation, or world
> to which I can connect my presentation?

———————

Clergy and lay church leaders regularly give presentations, such as sermons or reports. Roman Catholic priest Michael White suggests a question that may give great discipline and direction to their presentations:

> In one sentence, can you tell your congregation
> (or another group) what you want them to know
> and what you want them to do?

———————

Leaders often prepare articles or announcements related to their work. Questions to keep in mind in preparing such information might be:

> Why am I sharing this material?
> Who is the audience?
> What is the goal of this effort?
> How can I connect with the interests and values
> of the primary audience?

CREATIVE ABANDONMENT QUESTIONS

The Rev. Adam Hamilton of Leawood, Kansas, said that reopening of church programs following the pandemic was essentially a restart. It afforded an awesome opportunity to ask three questions:

> What needs to stop?
> What needs to continue?
> What needs to change?

Churches do many good things and tend always to add new things to an already full array of efforts. One way to spark thinking is to ask a group of leaders to assume that each of them has been hired as a consultant for the church. Provide them with a list of all the church's programs. Ask each of them to answer the question below and then talk about the church programs they chose and what they learned from this exercise:

> Based on our mission and what you know about the effectiveness
> of our programs to accomplish that mission, which programs
> would you recommend to (1) continue, (2) stop, or (3) change?

As with all organizations, churches develop many of their own rules. From time to time, it is good to gather staff and volunteer leaders to examine those taken for granted procedures with this question:

> If you could eliminate or change one rule (procedure, practice,
> report, etc.) that would help you do your ministry better,
> what would it be?

"We are eager to give birth to new ministries, but are lousy at letting old ones die," says Eddy Hall. He suggests a question church leaders can use each year to help ensure they are not over programming:

> What ministry program have you ended this year?

Robert I. Sutton and Huggy Rao describe a "subtraction game" in which an organization discovers things to eliminate in order to save time and energy for more productive uses. It starts with asking all participants to think about how their organization operates and answer these questions:

> What adds needless frustration?
> What scatters your attention?
> What was once useful but is now in the way?

Lee Kricher suggests that programs and practices that have outlived their usefulness can actually take away from a church's current mission. He suggests this question:

> What things *should* we eliminate that are real or potential distractions to our ability to fulfill our God-given vision?

EVENTS QUESTIONS

When thinking about a new endeavor, teams or committees often brainstorm and share ideas for addressing the opportunity or challenge at hand. One way to expand the group's knowledge base is to ask each person this question:

Before we meet again, will you identify and talk with one person
who is a potential participant for our new effort
and report back what you learn?

———————

Achieving a goal or preparing for an event requires many people doing
their work well. Often, mistakes are made and momentum lost when suf-
ficient time is not given to regular check-ins for the group, using questions
such as:

What's exciting about what you are doing?
What causes you to worry?
How is your workload?
What feedback would help you?
What suggestions would help the group?

———————

Leaders regularly need to decide who should be involved in planning an
event or initiative. Those for whom the effort is planned are logical participants, as well as persons who may have some experience or expertise
relevant to the subject of the enterprise. While people in formal leadership
positions are part of the planning, two more specific questions may help,
especially if there is any doubt about how the project may turn out:

Who is the person most at risk if things go wrong?
Who must answer questions if things don't work out?

———————

Over the course of a year, a congregation will provide a range of ongoing or one-time efforts to engage members and newcomers. Dan Pezet suggests that churches look back over all these efforts and ask these questions:

> Which initiative generated the most excitement in the church?
> Which initiative generated the most community support
> and participation?
> Was there an initiative that just felt natural to the church?

When a group seems frustrated in planning a project, questions that help to re-center are:

> What is the central goal of this task?
> What do we hope to accomplish?

When an event or ministry seems to have lost its vitality and becomes harder each year to implement successfully, it may be time to ask these questions:

> What need brought it into existence?
> What was its purpose when it began?
> Does that need still exist?
> If so, do the results from what we are currently doing indicate
> we are meeting the need well?

PLANNING QUESTIONS

Dwight Zscheile, Michael Binder, and Tessa Pinkstaff, in *Leading Faithful Innovation*, encourage church leaders to move away from asking "church questions" such as "How do we fix our church?" to asking "God questions" such as:

> What might God be up to in the lives of our neighbors?
> Where had God been present in the history of our congregation?
> How might the Spirit be moving in the lives
> of our members and neighbors?

Making plans that involve people other than those making the plans can be fraught with uncertainty and erroneous assumptions. Mike Bonem offers a question most groups can use regularly to address this dilemma:

> Who is not in the room that we should be thinking about?

When leaders and groups determine there is a need for a new ministry or improvement in an existing ministry, discussion turns quickly to what steps need to be taken. A prior question may be more important in determining if the "soil" is prepared in order for this endeavor to "bear fruit."

> What are the conditions required or conducive to make
> such a ministry most likely to flourish?

When a new challenge arises, our tendency is often to begin with the question, "What should we do?" If you already knew what to do, chances are someone would have done it already. The first task may be to learn more before doing anything. To gain that knowledge, you might ask questions such as these:

> With whom do we need to talk?
> Who else is facing this challenge?
> Who has experience in what we are facing?
> What internal and external information do we need to gather?

On a calendar, many activities may seem the same. However, every church expends its time and energy disproportionately across those efforts. These questions may provide clues about church priorities.

> What activities and ministries do we plan extensively?
> What activities and ministries do we plan very little?

Attempting a new ministry or a ministry for which you have no track record requires a different set of questions than those you might ask when attempting to improve an existing ministry. Some of the questions for a new ministry effort include:

> Does this ministry fit our mission and values?
> Is it feasible in light of our strengths and capabilities?
> Does it meet an important need?
> Are we clear about those we seek to reach and serve?
> What do we need to learn and with whom should we be talking?
> Is there a way to test our initial ideas and plans?
> On what assumptions are we basing our plans?

PROPERTY/FACILITIES QUESTIONS

Security for children's areas in the church is receiving increasing attention. Greg Atkinson visits many churches to help them see things as an outsider that the churches may be overlooking. Questions he asks as he reviews children's space include these related to safety:

> How easy is it to get to the nursery, classrooms,
> or child bathrooms?
> Is there a proper ratio of children's workers to children?
> Do the children get escorted out of the classroom
> and to the bathroom?
> Is there a back exit or entrance where children can go outside?
> Is it secure?

About once a year, gather together those responsible for the church facilities and those most directly related to reaching new people. Ask them to walk through all the church grounds and buildings on their own (not in groups) and make two lists based on these questions:

> What things do you see that would be welcoming
> for a new person?
> What things do you see that would not be welcoming
> for a new person?

Church leaders are always considering how to best use their property and facilities. Dave Harder suggests questions to consider:

Whom are our property and buildings for?
What are the dreams of our neighbors?
How could our building be an intersection of community
and connection in our neighborhood?

Gerald W. Keucher offers a question useful for church leaders when a congregation is making changes to facilities, but it would serve well for all decisions. He encourages use of this "successor test" question:

Will our successors thank us for doing this project this way?
Or will they mutter, "What were they thinking?"

While "All Are Welcome" messages abound outside churches, Carey Nieuwhof says that "increasingly unchurched people think about walking into a church the way you might think about randomly walking into a wedding to which you weren't invited." Convinced that in the future about the only way non-Christians will enter churches is through personal invitation, he suggests that the next time you drive by a church building you ask:

What would it take to convince me that I can walk in uninvited
and participate in what they're doing?

TECHNOLOGY QUESTIONS

As you are planning your website or reviewing your current website, you would do well to make sure these basic questions are answered:

What is our vision for our constituents and community?
What is it like here?
What can people expect?
How are we serving?
How can you connect?

Hayim Herring and Terri Martinson Elton share questions groups should consider if they plan to gather input through crowdsourcing:

What are the potential benefits and limitations
of crowdsourcing this idea?
What social media tools would you use?
How would you separate good ideas from bad ideas?
How would you communicate the results?

Today most new people encounter your church first through its website. Many church websites will benefit by regularly asking people having different connections with the church to view your website and offer feedback to a few questions regarding the site, such as:

Who appears to be the primary audience?
How would you describe its appearance?
How would you describe its tone?
What appears to be the primary purpose?
How easy is it to use?
Did you find outdated things or errors/typos?
What suggestions or advice would you offer
to improve our website?

Will Rice explores how technology can enhance ministry in congregations using some "what if" questions:

> What if someone traveling for business could check in with their small group during the week using video conference?
> What if someone who can no longer come to church could still be a part of their Sunday school class by using the technology?
> What if someone who can't get to the church during the work week could make an appointment to talk to a pastor or staff member via video conference?

USE OF TIME QUESTIONS

Leaders must generate much content each month. This may include sermons, lessons, devotionals, reports, updates, and announcements. Most are used once for the original purpose and put aside. In the digital and social media era, leaders might look at what they produce and ask:

> Are there versions of this (all, excerpts, quotations, statistics, etc.) that could be shared in other forms with a broader audience through social media, ebooks, or in other ways?

Leaders encounter many people from the church and community each week. If there is an opportunity for general conversation, instead of talking about the weather, wise leaders always have questions ready such as:

> What changes are you seeing in our community (or church)?
> What drew you to this community (or church)?
> What needs are you noticing in our community (or church)?

Many programs or events appear to have only one purpose. However, attentive leaders understand that a special occurrence can usually serve multiple goals and purposes. These questions may help you think of ancillary benefits of programs and events:

> Who in the community needs to know about this
> because of the subject?
> Who in the community might be interested
> because of the speakers or leaders?
> Are there key church or community leaders to invite
> to meet some of the speakers or leaders?

———————

Leaders need to reflect on their use of time by asking questions to help view their commitments in light of their responsibilities as a leader. Questions that may help include:

> What are those things that can only be done by me
> because of my role and position?
> What are those things that people have a right to expect of me
> that, if I do not do them, no one else can
> or in all likelihood will do them?
> What are those things that can only be done
> in the current time period?

———————

Leaders face a never-ending flow of requests. Bruce Tulgan offers ways leaders can be responsive to these requests while avoiding a premature "yes." He suggests these questions may give you information you need to decide while also conveying how seriously you take such commitments:

> Who is the asker, and do you have the person
> or group's approval?
> What is the deliverable being requested?
> By when does it need to be accomplished?
> What resources will be required?
> What are the possible benefits?
> What are the obvious and hidden costs?

It is common in churches to say that our budget acknowledges our priorities. How we spend our financial resources surely represents our values in a practical way. However, there is another indicator of our priorities. Our use of time is an even more accurate indication of values; yet seldom is attention given to the "time budget" of how our members, staff, and pastors are asked by the church to spend their time. A good question may simply be:

> How do we allocate our time and ask others
> to allocate their time?

In Times of Transition

Times of transition are occasions of great opportunity and risk, and such transitions are difficult both for leaders and organizations experiencing the changes. Mistakes are easily made in such times as long-time practices and relationships prove inadequate or even inappropriate. Sometimes the tasks associated with transition overshadow the emotional and spiritual dimensions that always accompany change—dimensions that are critical to living through any transition.

TRANSITION QUESTIONS

When a new pastor arrives, it can sometimes be frustrating to hear church members talk so much about their previous pastor and even earlier pastors. It is as if the congregation wants to focus backwards just when the new pastor is trying to guide things toward the future. But progress usually grows out of heritage and shared values. Rather than being defensive regarding talk of predecessor pastors, the new pastor can use this request to reveal much about the congregation:

> Tell me about some of your favorite former pastors
> and why you remember them so fondly.

Getting started in a new role or place can be a challenge for leaders. While you want to respect current practices, you also want to use this moment as a chance to encourage creative alternatives. Terry J. Fadem suggests these questions regarding a current church practice or problem:

> How does this work?
> What do I need to know about this now that I'm here?
> Who else might be able to help us?
> How has this problem been resolved before?
> Who has the most experience tackling this problem?

Despite a range of diversity represented by effective leaders, Peter Drucker found that they behaved in much the same way. They asked similar questions. For example, when going into a new position, instead of asking "What do I want?" or "What do I want to do?" they asked these questions:

> What are the organization's mission and goals?
> What needs to be done?
> What can and should I do to make a difference?

When new pastors arrive, they need ways to learn much about a new church in a short time. Jim Ozier and Jim Griffith suggest giving members notecards and asking them to write their responses to these questions:

> What is one thing I need to know about the church?
> What is one way we are going to reach new people?
> What is one dream you have for the church?

Mark Edington tells of a congregation that was moving from having a full-time pastor to having a bivocational pastor who would serve the church part time while having other employment. The congregation and incoming pastor found these two questions helped them make important decisions about the role of the pastor in this new configuration:

> What do you expect the pastor to do?
> How necessary is it for a pastor to do that?

Notes

Introduction

1. Andrew Young, *An Easy Burden* (New York: HarperCollins, 1996), 326.

Reflections on Question Asking: Why Ask Questions

1. Peter Drucker, quoted in Gary B. Cohen, *Just Ask Leadership: Why Great Managers Always Ask the Right Questions* (New York: McGraw-Hill, 2009), 8.

2. David Brooks, *How to Know a Person: The Art of Seeing Others Deeply and Being Deeply Seen* (New York: Random House, 2023), 85.

3. Edgar H. Schein, *Humble Inquiry: The Gentle Art of Asking Instead of Telling* (San Francisco: Berrett-Koehler, 2013), 3–4.

Personal Reflection and Growth

Robin Diangelo, *Nice Racism: How Progressive White People Perpetuate Racial Harm* (Boston: Beacon, 2021) 177.

John Mark Comer, *The Ruthless Elimination of Hurry* (New York: Penguin Random House, 2019), 6.

Saj-nicole A. Joni, *The Third Opinion: How Successful Leaders Use Outside Insight to Create Superior Results* (New York: Penguin, 2004), 179.

James R. Hagerty, *Yours Truly: An Obituary Writer's Guide to Telling Your Story* (New York: Kensington, 2023), xii.

Jacqui Lewis, *Fierce Love* (New York: Penguin Random House, 2021), 45–46.

Hans Küng, *Why Priests? A Proposal for a New Church Ministry* (Garden City, NY: Doubleday, 1972), 117.

"What Are Our Values? An interview with Carlos Correa Bernier," Yale Divinity School *Reflections*, Fall 2016, 29.

Robert Bruce Shaw and Mark Ronald, "Changing Culture—Patience is Not a Virtue," *Leader to Leader*, Fall 2012, 51.

Rosabeth Moss Kanter, *Think Outside the Building: How Advanced Leaders Can Change the World One Smart Innovation at a Time* (New York: Public Affairs, 2020), 120.

Justin A. Irving and Mark L. Strauss, *Leadership in Christian Perspective* (Grand Rapids: Baker Academic, 2019), 51.

Carey Nieuwhof, "7 Questions That Can Help You Crush a Plateau and Gain Momentum," February 16, 2017, http://careynieuwhof.com/7-questions-that-can-help-you-crush-a-plateau-and-gain-momentum/?mc_cid=b47c4f95a1&mc_eid=1952abcca7.

Carey Nieuwhof, "3 Quick Ways to See How Effective Your Leadership Really Is," https://careynieuwhof.com/3-quick-ways-to-see-how-effective-your-leadership-really-is/.

Gaining Perspective

Alban Weekly newsletter, November 9, 2020.

Shawn Stewart, "6 Critical Questions to Ask Before Renaming Your Church," https://tonymorganlive.com/2018/11/19/6-critical-questions-church-name-change/?utm_campaign=%5BMQL%20to%20SQL%5D&utm_source=hs_email&utm_medium=email&utm_content=67674122&_hsenc=p2ANqtz-_LNU-rSmLhUZWS_9dkuep9YeCo-k8eAmFmI_m6Z3ztJbpdyIQ-_MLMpHhDKtWGsJU6XNDCfbks74r78HiVD7zeAb1gsK7mg0uvM_zvXIW-_igHWfc&_hsmi=67674601. Tony Morgan Live (https://tonymorganlive.com), November 19, 2018.

James A. Harnish, *Extraordinary Ministry in Ordinary Time: An Invitation to Renewal for Pastors* (Nashville: Abingdon Press, 2019), 72.

Kay Kotan and Blake Bradford, *Impact: Reclaiming the Call of Lay Ministry* (Knoxville, TN: Market Square, 2018), 86.

Lee Kricher, *For a New Generation: A Practical Guide for Revitalizing Your Church* (Grand Rapids: Zondervan, 2016), 55.

Alan J. Roxburgh, *Joining God, Remaking Church, Changing the World: The New Shape of the Church in Our Time* (New York: Morehouse, 2015), 72.

Rich Birch, "5 Lessons Church Leaders Can Learn From The 'All-Day Breakfast' Trend," October 16, 2018, https://unseminary.com/5-lessons -church-leaders-can-learn-from-the-all-day-breakfast-trend/.

Michael White and Tom Corcoran, *Tools for Rebuilding* (Notre Dame, IN: Ave Maria Press, 2013), 46.

Bob Smietana, *Reorganized Religion: The Reshaping of the American Church and Why It Matters* (New York: Worthy, 2022), 91.

Greg Atkinson, *Secrets of a Secret Shopper: Reaching and Keeping Church Guests* (Nashville: Rainer Publishing, 2016), 86.

Gil Rendle, *Quietly Courageous: Leading the Church in a Changing World* (Lanham, MD: Rowman & Littlefield, 2019), 72.

Charles Zech, "White Paper on US Catholic Parish Management: Building the Parish Business Model for the 21st Century," *U.S. Catholic Management*, date unknown, perhaps 2014.

Reflections on Question Asking: Questions Build Trust

1. Quoted in Andrew Sobel and Jerold Panas, *Power Questions: Build Relationships, Win New Business, and Influence Others* (New York: John Wiley & Sons, 2012), 14.

2. Robin Lovin, Wisconsin Pastors' School, 1993.

3. Brooks, *How to Know a Person*, 87.

Making Good Decisions

Andy Stanley, *Better Decisions, Fewer Regrets: 5 Questions to Help You Determine Your Next Move* (Grand Rapids: Zondervan, 2020), 137.

Ursula M. Burns, *Where You Are Is Not Who You Are: A Memoir* (New York: HarperCollins, 2021), 159.

Mary Parker Follett, "The Giving of Orders," in Henry C. Metcalf, ed., *Scientific Foundations of Business Administration* (Baltimore, MD: Williams & Wilkins, 1926), 29–37.

Jeff Bezos, *Invent and Wander: The Collected Writings of Jeff Bezos* (Boston: Harvard Business Review Press, 2021), 227–29.

Molly Phinney Baskette, *How to Begin When Your World Is Ending: A Spiritual Field Guide to Joy Despite Everything* (Minneapolis: Broadleaf, 2022), 207.

George B. Thompson, Jr., *How to Get Along with Your Pastor* (Cleveland, OH: Pilgrim, 2006), 39.

Susan MacKenty Brady, Janet Foutty, and Lynn Perry Wooten, *Arrive and Thrive: 7 Impactful Practices for Women Navigating Leadership* (New York: McGraw Hill, 2022), 73.

Hayim Herring and Terri Martinson Elton, *Leading Congregations and Nonprofits in a Connected World: Platforms, People, and Purpose* (Lanham, MD: Rowman & Littlefield, 2017), 131.

Julia Binder and Michael D. Watkins, "To Solve a Tough Problem, Reframe It," *Harvard Business Review* (January-February 2024), 87–88.

Mónica Guzmán, *I Never Thought of It That Way* (Dallas: BenBella, 2022), 134.

Chloe Maxmim and Canyon Woodward, *Dirt Road Revival: How to Rebuild Rural Politics and Why Our Future Depends on It* (Boston, MA: Beacon Press, 2022), 95.

Adam Grant, *Think Again: The Power of Knowing What You Don't Know* (New York: Viking, 2021), 254.

Mónica Guzmán, *I Never Thought of It That Way* (Dallas: BenBella, 2022), 49.

Justo L. González, ed., *Each in Our Own Tongue: A History of Hispanic United Methodism* (Nashville: Abingdon Press, 1991), 156–57.

Thomas G. Kirkpatrick, *Communication in the Church: A Handbook for Healthier Relationships* (Lanham, MD: Rowman & Littlefield, 2016), 72.

Working with Others

Debi Nixon, Leading Ideas Talks podcast, Lewis Center for Church Leadership, www.churchleadership.com, summer, 2020.

Hayim Herring and Terri Martinson Elton, *Leading Congregations and Nonprofits in a Connected World: Platforms, People, and Purpose* (Lanham, MD: Rowman & Littlefield, 2017), 91.

Rick Rusaw and Brian Mavis, *The Neighboring Church: Getting Better at What Jesus Said Matters Most* (Nashville: Thomas Nelson, 2016), 126.

Andrew Sobel and Jerold Panas, *Power Questions Build Relationship, Win New Business, and Influence Others* (New York: Wiley, 2012), 186.

Lee Kricher, *Seamless Pastoral Transition: 3 Imperatives—6 Pitfalls* (Maitland, FL: Xulon, 2022), 33.

Carey Nieuwhof, "7 Questions Every Volunteer Asks," https://careynieuwhof.com/7-questions-every-volunteer-asks/.

Robert Schnase, *Just Say Yes! Unleashing People for Ministry* (Nashville: Abingdon Press, 2015), 64–65.

Brandon P. Fleming, *Miseducated: A Memoir* (New York: Hachette, 2021), 251.

Keith Ferrazzi, "A New Social Contract for Teams," *Harvard Business Review* (September–October 2022), 92.

Donna Claycomb Sokol and L. Roger Owens, *A New Day in the City: Urban Church Renewal* (Nashville: Abingdon Press, 2017), 136–37.

Adam Grant, *Think Again: The Power of Knowing What You Don't Know* (New York: Viking, 2021), 211.

Eric Hoeke, "Building a Healthy Church Leadership Team," Pittsburgh Theological Seminary blog, July 19, 2022.

Thomas G. Kirkpatrick, *Communication in the Church: A Handbook for Healthier Relationships* (Lanham, MD: Rowman & Littlefield, 2016), 34.

Reflections on Question Asking: Right Questions Help Communicate Values and Priorities

1. Alicia Garza, *The Purpose of Power: How We Come Together When We Fall Apart* (New York: One World, 2020), 94.

2. Garza, *The Purpose of Power*, 94

3. Brian Grazer, *A Curious Mind: The Secret to a Bigger Life* (New York: Simon & Schuster, 2015), 144.

4. Peter Senge, "Excerpts from 'Mastering the Tools of Change,'" *Drucker Foundation News*, March 1998, 5.

Making a Difference

Chris McChesney, Sean Covey, and Jim Huling, *The 4 Disciplines of Execution: Achieving Your Wildly Important Goals* (New York: Free Press, 2012), 143.

Tony Morgan, *The Unstuck Church: Equipping Churches to Experience Sustained Health* (Nashville: Thomas Nelson, 2017), 97.

Howard Stevenson, *Getting to Giving: Fundraising the Entrepreneurial Way* (Belmont, MA: Timberline LLC, 2011), 68.

Paul Harvey, *Martin Luther King: A Religious Life* (Lanham, MD: Rowman & Littlefield, 2021), 101.

James A. Harnish, *Extraordinary Ministry in Ordinary Time: An Invitation to Renewal for Pastors* (Nashville: Abingdon Press, 2019), 71.

Charles Marsh and John Perkins, *Welcoming Justice: God's Movement Toward Beloved Community* (Downers Grove, IL: IVP Books, 2009), 41.

Charles Zech, "White Paper on US Catholic Parish Management: Building the Parish Business Model for the 21st Century," *U.S. Catholic Management*, date unknown, perhaps 2014.

Gerald H. Kennedy, *The Preacher and the New English Bible* (New York: Oxford University Press, 1972), 68.

Peter F. Drucker, "Managing Oneself," *Drucker Foundation News* (January 2000), vol. 8, issue 1, 6.

Review and Assessment

Robert H. Rosen, *Leading People: Transforming Business from the Inside Out* (New York: Viking, 1996), 52.

Alicia Garza, *The Purpose of Power: How We Come Together When We Fall Apart* (New York: One World, 2020), 4.

Rich Birch, "5 Lessons Church Leaders Can Learn From The 'All-Day Breakfast' Trend," October 16, 2018, https://unseminary.com/5-lessons-church-leaders-can-learn-from-the-all-day-breakfast-trend/.

Vijay Govindarajan and Chris Trimble, *The Other Side of Innovation: Solving the Execution Challenge* (Boston: Harvard Business Review Press, 2010), 114.

Dan Pezet, *Expanding the Expedition Through Community Connection* (Knoxville, TN: Market Square, 2021), 17.

Margaret J. Wheatley, *Who Do We Choose to Be? Facing Reality, Claiming Leadership, Restoring Sanity* (San Francisco: Berrett-Koehler, 2017), 132.

Paul Polman and Andrew Winston, "The Net Positive Manifesto: Is the World Better Off Because Your Company is in It," *Harvard Business Review* (September–October 2021), 125.

Ozan Varol, *Think Like a Rocket Scientist: Simple Strategies You Can Use to Make Giant Leaps in Work and Life* (New York: Public Affairs, 2020), 235.

David Michels and Kevin Murphy, "How Good Is Your Company at Change?" *Harvard Business Review* (July–August 2021), 70.

Tony Morgan, "How Cokesbury UMC Asks the Right Questions about Church Health," interview with Pastor Stephen DeFur, TonyMorganLive.com, March 29, 2016.

David Hull, "By the Numbers," http://chchurches.org/blog/, April 12, 2016.

Carey Nieuwhof, "5 Smarter Ways to Embrace Infrequent Church Attenders," https://careynieuwhof.com/5-smarter-ways-to-embrace-infrequent-church-attenders/.

Reflections on Question Asking: Questions Address the Challenge of Competing Values

1. Andrew Sobel and Jerold Panas, *Power Questions: Build Relationships, Win New Business, and Influence Others* (New York: John Wiley & Sons, 2012), 4.

Leading Change

Shawn Lovejoy, *Be Mean about the Vision: Preserving and Protecting What Matters* (Nashville: Thomas Nelson, 2016), 10.

Vashti Murphy McKenzie, *Strength in the Struggle: Leadership Development for Women* (Cleveland, OH: Pilgrim, 2001), 6–7.

Robert Mai and Alan Akerson, *The Leader as Communicator: Strategies and Tactics to Build Loyalty, Focus Effort, and Spark Creativity* (New York: American Management Association, 2003), 70.

James A. Harnish, *Extraordinary Ministry in Ordinary Time: An Invitation to Renewal for Pastors* (Nashville: Abingdon Press, 2019), 120.

Scott Cormode, *The Innovative Church: How Leaders and Their Congregations Can Adapt in an Ever-Changing World* (Grand Rapids: Baker Academic, 2020), 173. I also thank Scott for his wonderful definition of leadership that is captured in multiple questions that use the phrase "next faithful step." His definition of church leadership is "helping God's people take their next faithful step." See Lovett H. Weems, Jr., *Take the Next Step: Leading Lasting Change in the Church* (Nashville: Abingdon Press, 2003).

Ronald Heifetz, *Leadership Without Easy Answers* (Cambridge, MA: Belknap Press, 1994), 242.

Minal Bopaiah, *Equity: How to Design Organizations Where Everyone Thrives* (San Francisco: Berrett-Koehler, 2021), 42.

Joseph Steinberg, "Should Beth Implement Facial Recognition Software at the Cub House: The Experts Respond," *Harvard Business Review* (November–December 2022), 148.

Jim Tomberlin and Warren Bird, *Better Together: Making Church Mergers Work,* expanded and updated edition (Minneapolis: Fortress, 2020), 24.

Robert T. Handy, *A History of Union Theological Seminary in New York* (New York: Columbia University Press, 1987), 191.

Susan Beaumont, "10 Questions to Ask Now," June 19, 2020, https://susanbeaumont.com/2020/06/19/10-questions-to-ask-now/.

Gil Rendle, *Quietly Courageous: Leading the Church in a Changing World* (Lanham, MD: Rowman & Littlefield, 2019), 9.

Alan J. Roxburgh, *Structured for Mission: Renewing the Culture of the Church* (Downers Grove, IL: IVP Books, 2015), 146.

Innovation
Adam Grant, *Think Again: The Power of Knowing What You Don't Know* (New York: Viking, 2021), 210–11.

Tod Bolsinger, *Tempered Resilience: How Leaders Are Formed in the Crucible of Change* (Downers Grove, IL: InterVarsity Press, 2020), 15.

Vijay Govindarajan and Chris Trimble, *The Other Side of Innovation: Solving the Execution Challenge* (Boston: Harvard Business Review Press, 2010), 112.

Fernando F. Suarez and Juan S. Montes, "Building Organizational Resilience," *Harvard Business Review* (November–December 2020), 52.

Sydney Finkelstein, *Why Smart Executives Fail* (New York: Penguin, 2003), 200.

Rich Birch, "7 Strategic Questions Churches Need to Ask about Reopening," May 5, 2020, https://unseminary.com/7-strategic-questions-churches-need-to-ask-about-reopening/.

Will Mancini and Warren Bird, *God's Dreams: 12 Vision Templates for Finding and Focusing Your Church's Future* (Nashville: B & H Publishing, 2016), 81.

Dwight Zscheile, *The Agile Church: Spirit-Led Innovation in an Uncertain Age* (New York: Morehouse, 2014), 88.

Michael Frost and Alan Hirsch, *The Shaping of Things to Come: Innovation and Mission for the 21st Century Church*, rev. ed. (Grand Rapids: Baker Books, 2013), 237.

Saj-nicole A. Joni, *The Third Opinion: How Successful Leaders Use Outside Insight to Create Superior Results* (New York: Penguin, 2004), 171, 179.

Reflections on Question Asking: Questions Lead to Discoveries

1. Martin B. Copenhaver, *Jesus Is the Question: The 307 Questions Jesus Asked and the 3 He Answered* (Nashville: Abingdon Press, 2014), xvii–xviii.

2. Thomas Merton, *The Seven Storey Mountain: An Autobiography of Faith* (New York: Harcourt, 1948), 154.

Expanding Reach and Impact

"Faith, Reform, and the Needs of the Living," Yale Divinity School *Reflections*, Fall 2017, 28.

Tony Morgan, *The Unstuck Church: Equipping Churches to Experience Sustained Health* (Nashville: Thomas Nelson, 2017), 111.

Michael Frost and Alan Hirsch, *The Shaping of Things to Come: Innovation and Mission for the 21st Century Church*, rev. ed. (Grand Rapids: Baker, 2013), 237.

"What I've Never Seen," J. Clif Christopher, *Money & Ministry* online newsletter, November 2013, Horizons Stewardship.

Dan Pezet, *Expanding the Expedition Through Community Connection* (Knoxville, TN: Market Square Publishing, 2021), 31.

Michael White and Tom Corcoran, *Tools for Rebuilding* (Notre Dame, IN: Ave Maria Press, 2013), 26.

Rich Birch, "Should You Even Bother Worrying about Church Growth?" unSeminary blog, January 15, 2019, unSeminary.com.

F. Douglas Powe, Jr., *New Wine, New Wineskins: How African American Congregations Can Reach New* Generations (Nashville: Abingdon Press, 2012), 83.

James Hudnut-Beumler, "The Quakerization of Mainline Protestantism," in *The Future of Mainline Protestantism in America*, ed. James Hudnut-Beumler and Mark Silk (New York: Columbia University Press, 2018), 181.

Rich Birch, "10 Questions Church Leaders Should Be Asking but Probably Aren't" (July 20, 2018), http://www.unseminary.com/10-questions-church-leaders-should-be-asking-but-probably-arent/.

Carey Nieuwhof, *Lasting Impact: 7 Powerful Conversations That Will Help Your Church Grow* (Cumming, GA: The rethink Group, 2015), 24.

David Olshine, *Youth Ministry: What's Gone Wrong and How to Get It Right* (Nashville: Abingdon Press, 2013), 27.

Kara Powell, Jen Bradbury, Brad Griffin, *Faith Beyond Youth Group: 5 Ways to Form Character and Cultivate Lifelong Discipleship* (Grand Rapids: Baker, 2023), 103–04.

Rick Rusaw and Brian Mavis, *The Neighboring Church: Getting Better at What Jesus Said Matters Most* (Nashville: Thomas Nelson, 2016), 14.

Molly Phinney Baskette, *Real Good Church: How Our Church Came Back from the Dead, and Yours Can*, Too (Cleveland, OH: Pilgrim, 2014), 80.

Church Ministries

Lee Kricher, *For a New Generation: A Practical Guide for Revitalizing Your Church* (Grand Rapids: Zondervan, 2016), 38.

Lee Kricher, *For a New Generation: A Practical Guide for Revitalizing Your Church* (Grand Rapids: Zondervan, 2016), 55.

Gil Rendle, "Leading a Congregation Through Change," 2002 Calvin Symposium on Worship and the Arts, Calvin Institute of Christian Worship, January 11, 2002.

Bill Easum and Bill Tenny-Brittian, *Ministry in Hard Times* (Nashville: Abingdon Press, 2010), 87.

Charles Marsh and John Perkins, *Welcoming Justice: God's Movement Toward Beloved Community* (Downers Grove, IL: IVP Books, 2009), 48.

Rosario Picardo, *Funding Ministry with Five Loaves and Two Fishes* (Nashville: Abingdon Press, 2016), 88–89.

Rick Rusaw and Eric Swanson, *The Externally Focused Church* (Loveland, CO: Group Publishing, 2004), 90.

Nelson Searcy, *The Renegade: Abandoning Average in Your Life and Ministry* (Grand Rapids: Baker, 2013), 123.

Jacob Armstrong, *Treasure: A Four-Week Stewardship Program, Devotional Readings* (Nashville: Abingdon Press, 2014).

Alban Weekly newsletter, September 15, 2020.

F. Douglas Powe, Jr., *New Wine, New Wineskins: How African American Congregations Can Reach New Generations* (Nashville: Abingdon Press, 2012), xii.

Matt Miofsky and Jason Byassee, *8 Virtues of Rapidly Growing Churches* (Nashville: Abingdon Press, 2018), 20.

Gordon D. Kaufman, *In the Face of Mystery: A Constructive Theology* (Cambridge, MA: Harvard University Press, 1993), 15.

John Wesley, "Minutes of Several Conversations" (also known as the "Large Minutes"), Question 50, *The Works of the Rev. John Wesley, A.M.,* ed. Thomas Jackson, 3rd ed. (London: John Mason, 1831), 8:324–35.

Tod Bolsinger, *Tempered Resilience: How Leaders Are Formed in the Crucible of Change* (Downers Grove, IL: InterVarsity Press, 2020), 199.

Erin Weber-Johnson, "Who Is Giving? Part 2," October 23, 2018, https://faithlead.org/blog/who-is-giving-part-2/.

Mike Slaughter, *The Christian Wallet: Spending, Giving, and Living with a Conscience* (Louisville, KY: Westminster John Knox, 2016), 33.

Margaret J. Marcuson, *Money and Your Ministry: Balance the Books While Keeping Your Balance* (Portland: Marcuson Leadership Circle, 2014), 56–57.

Howard Stevenson, *Getting to Giving: Fundraising the Entrepreneurial Way* (Belmont, MA: Timberline LLC, 2011), 15.

Charlie Baber, "Oh, Because YOUR Worship Wars Are SO Much More Relevant," *United Methodist Insight,* September 13, 2022, https://um-insight .net/perspectives/oh-because-your-worship-wars-are-so-much-more -relevant/.

Michael White and Tom Corcoran, *Rebuilt: Awakening the Faithful, Reaching the Lost, Making Church Matter* (Notre Dame, IN: Ave Maria Press, 2013), 93–105.

James Lemler, *Transforming Congregations* (New York: Church Publishing, 2008), 97–98.

Reflections on Question Asking: Use Questions for Insight and Not for Blame

1. Max De Pree, *Leadership is an Art* (New York: Crown Currency, 2004) 58.

Community Concerns

G. Travis Norvell, *Church on the Move: A Practical Guide for Ministry in the Community* (Valley Forge, PA: Judson Press, 2022), 32.

Mark Mogilka and Kate Wiskus, *Pastoring Multiple Parishes* (Chicago: Loyola, 2009), 29.

George B. Thompson, Jr., *How to Get Along with Your Pastor* (Cleveland, OH: Pilgrim, 2006), 39.

G. Travis Norvell, *Church on the Move: A Practical Guide for Ministry in the Community* (Valley Forge, PA: Judson, 2022), 11.

Luke S. Edwards, *Becoming Church: A Trail Guide for Starting Fresh Expressions* (Richmond, VA: Fresh Expressions, 2021), 51.

Dave Harder, "Reimaging Church Buildings: From Liability to Asset," Dustin D. Benac and Erin Weber-Johnson, eds., *Crisis & Care: Meditations on Faith and Philanthropy* (Eugene, OR: Cascade, 2021), 83.

Adam Grant, *Think Again: The Power of Knowing What You Don't Know* (New York: Viking, 2021), 122–23.

Alicia Garza, *The Purpose of Power: How We Come Together When We Fall Apart* (New York: One World, 2020), 91.

Kevin Murriel, presentation at Leadership Institute, Resurrection, a United Methodist Church, Leawood, Kansas, 2021.

Robin Diangelo, *Nice Racism: How Progressive White People Perpetuate Racial Harm* (Boston: Beacon, 2021), 8.

Ella F. Washington, "The Five Stages of DEI Maturity," *Harvard Business Review* (November–December 2022), 92–99.

Jacqui Lewis, *Fierce Love* (New York: Penguin Random House, 2021), 159–60.

Leslie Dunbar, "Homage to the Brave," in F. Thomas Trotter, ed., *Politics, Morality, and Higher Education: Essays in Honor of Samuel DuBois Cook* (Franklin, TN: Providence House, 1997), 88–89.

Robert D. Putnam and David E. Campbell, *American Grace: How Religion Divides and Unites Us* (New York: Simon & Schuster, 2010), 4.

Courtney E. Martin, *Learning in Public: Lessons for a Racially Divided America from My Daughter's School* (New York: Little, Brown, and Company, 2021), 84.

Susan MacKenty Brady, Janet Foutty, and Lynn Perry Wooten, *Arrive and Thrive: 7 Impactful Practices for Women Navigating Leadership* (New York: McGraw Hill, 2022), 172.

Michael R. Fisher, *Leading Ideas Talks* podcast, Lewis Center for Church Leadership, www.churchleadership.com, summer 2020.

Robert D. Putnam and David E. Campbell, *American Grace: How Religion Divides and Unites Us* (New York: Simon & Schuster, 2010), 7.

Charles Marsh and John Perkins, *Welcoming Justice: God's Movement Toward Beloved Community* (Downers Grove, IL: IVP Books, 2009), 41.

"This is what Southern Baptist Convention leaders are dishonoring when they embrace bigotry," *Washington Post*, June 10, 2021, https://www.washingtonpost.com/opinions/2021/06/10/russell-moore-sbc-christian-conscience/.

Michael R. Fisher, *Leading Ideas Talks* podcast, Lewis Center for Church Leadership, www.churchleadership.com, summer 2020.

Robert M. Franklin, *Crisis in the Village: Restoring Hope in African American Communities* (Minneapolis: Fortress, 2007), 214.

Personnel

Vijay Govindarajan and Chris Trimble, *The Other Side of Innovation: Solving the Execution Challenge* (Boston: Harvard Business Review Press, 2010), 115.

Peter F. Drucker, "Managing Oneself," *Drucker Foundation News* (January 2000), vol. 8, issue 1, 7.

Susan Beaumont, "Staff Team Design for a New Era," March 6, 2023, https://www.congregationalconsulting.org/staff-team-design-for-a-new-era/.

Deborah Ike, September 15, 2015, http://us4.campaign-archive2.com /?u=b6979e7b3ae3397ff211e73da&id=adbd04a4e6&e=da220afca4.

Frederick F. Reichheld, "The One Number You Need to Grow," *Harvard Business Review* (December 2003), 50.

David L. Dotlich and Peter C. Cairo, *Why CEOs Fail* (San Francisco: Jossey-Bass, 2003), xxii.

Dave Ulrich, "Credibility x Capability," *The Leader of the Future: New Visions, Strategies, and Practices for the Next Era*, eds. Frances Hesselbein, Marshall Goldsmith, and Richard Beckhard (San Francisco: Jossey-Bass, 1996), 217.

Robert Schnase, *Just Say Yes! Unleashing People for Ministry* (Nashville: Abingdon Press, 2015), 65.

Dave Ferguson and Warren Bird, *Hero Maker: Five Essential Practices for Leaders to Multiply Leaders* (Grand Rapids: Zondervan, 2018), 45.

Reflections on Question Asking: Ways to Enhance Your Question Asking

1. David Brooks, *How to Know a Person: The Art of Seeing Others Deeply and Being Deeply Seen* (New York: Random House, 2023), 85.

Management Skills

Dianna Booher, "10 Questions to Stellar Communication," *Leader to Leader* (Fall 2007), 42–48.

Scott D. Anthony, Clark G. Gilbert, and Mark W. Johnson, *Dual Transformation: How to Reposition Today's Business While Creating the Future* (Cambridge, MA: Harvard Business Review Press, 2017), 11.

Michael White and Tom Corcoran, *Tools for Rebuilding* (Notre Dame, IN: Ave Maria Press, 2013), 124.

Eddy Hall, Ray Bowman, and J. Skipp Machmer, *The More with Less Church: Maximize Your Money, Space, Time, and People to Multiply Ministry Impact* (Grand Rapids: Baker, 2014), 21–22.

Robert I. Sutton and Huggy Rao, "Rid Your Organization of Obstacles That Infuriate Everyone," *Harvard Business Review* (January–February 2024), 105.

Lee Kricher, *For a New Generation: A Practical Guide for Revitalizing Your Church* (Grand Rapids: Zondervan, 2016), 85–86.

Chloe Maxmim and Canyon Woodward, *Dirt Road Revival: How to Rebuild Rural Politics and Why Our Future Depends on It* (Boston: Beacon, 2022), 133.

Dan Pezet, *Expanding the Expedition Through Community Connection* (Knoxville, TN: Market Square, 2021), 56.

Dwight Zscheile, Michael Binder, and Tessa Pinkstaff, *Leading Faithful Innovation: Following God into a Hopeful Future* (Minneapolis: Fortress, 2023), 8, 39–40.

Mike Bonem, *The Art of Leading Change: Ten Perspectives on the Messiness of Ministry* (Minneapolis: Fortress, 2022), 6.

Greg Atkinson, *Secrets of a Secret Shopper: Reaching and Keeping Church Guests* (Nashville: Rainer, 2016), 94.

Dave Harder, "Reimaging Church Buildings: From Liability to Asset," in *Crisis & Care: Meditations on Faith and Philanthropy*, ed. Dustin D. Benac and Erin Weber-Johnson (Eugene, OR: Cascade, 2021), 83.

Gerald W. Keucher, *Humble and Strong: Mutually Accountable Leadership in the Church* (New York: Morehouse, 2010), 123.

Carey Nieuwhof, "10 Things that Demonstrate the World You Grew Up in No Longer Exists," December 28, 2016, Carey Nieuwhof blog, www.careynieuwhof.com.

Hayim Herring and Terri Martinson Elton, *Leading Congregations and Nonprofits in a Connected World: Platforms, People, and Purpose* (Lanham, MD: Rowman & Littlefield, 2017), 18.

Will Rice blog, www.pastorwill.net, August 25, 2015.

Bruce Tulgan, "Learn When to Say No . . . and How to Say Yes," *Harvard Business Review*, September–October 2020, 136–37.

In Times of Transition

Peter F. Drucker, "Foreword," *The Leader of the Future: New Visions, Strategies, and Practices for the Next Era*, ed. Frances Hesselbein, Marshall Goldsmith, and Richard Beckhard (San Francisco: Jossey-Bass, 1996), xiii.

Jim Ozier and Jim Griffith, *The Changeover Zone: Successful Pastoral Transitions* (Nashville: Abingdon Press, 2016), 69–71.

Mark D. W. Edington, *Bivocational: Returning to the Roots of Ministry* (New York: Church Publishing, 2018), 53.

Ready to go deeper with these questions?

Scan the QR code below or visit https://cokesbury.formtitan
.com/ftproject/therightquestionsforchurchleaders to read reflections
from fellow church leaders responding to Lovett Weems's
thought-provoking *Right Questions*.

https://cokesbury.formtitan.com/ftproject/therightquestionsforchurchleaders

Join the conversation!

This dialogue gets better when you're a part of it.
Share your thoughts in the comments section.
We look forward to hearing from you!

Ready to go deeper with these questions?

Scan the QR code below, or visit bhpublishinggroup.com to get
a free printable Bible conversation booklet that you send to your
two fellow church readers. Speak to your Covert Woman
thoughts or points, Ready reasons.

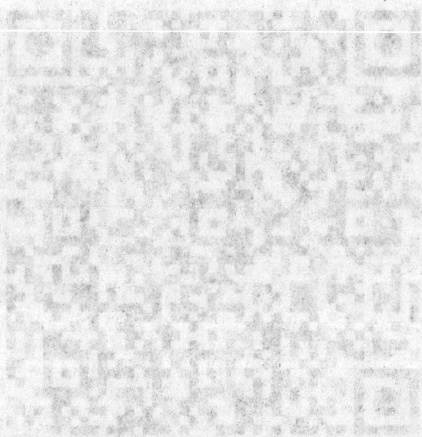

bhpublishinggroup.com/Image-critical/bible-conversation-book

Join the conversation.

The talking gets better when you're a part of it.
Share your thoughts with the community, and
we'd love to read or hearing from you.

www.ingramcontent.com/pod-product-compliance
Lightning Source LLC
Chambersburg PA
CBHW010041090426
42734CB00019B/3242

* 9 7 8 1 7 9 1 0 3 7 0 1 7 *